HOTSPOTS
MENORCA

Thomas Cook

Written by Tony Kelly, updated by Jane Egginton
Front cover photography courtesy of Thomas Cook Tour Operations Ltd

Original design concept by Studio 183 Limited
Series design by the Bridgewater Book Company
Cover design/artwork by Lee Biggadike, Studio 183 Limited

Produced by the Bridgewater Book Company
The Old Candlemakers, West Street, Lewes, East Sussex BN7 2NZ, United Kingdom
www.bridgewaterbooks.co.uk
Project Editor: Emily Casey Bailey
Project Designer: Lisa McCormick

Published by Thomas Cook Publishing
A division of Thomas Cook Tour Operations Limited
PO Box 227, Units 15-16, Coningsby Road, Peterborough PE3 8SB, United Kingdom
email: books@thomascook.com
www.thomascookpublishing.com
+ 44 (0) 1733 416477

ISBN-13: 978-1-84157-538-4
ISBN-10: 1-84157-538-0

First edition © 2006 Thomas Cook Publishing
Text © 2006 Thomas Cook Publishing
Maps © 2006 Thomas Cook Publishing
Head of Thomas Cook Publishing: Chris Young
Project Editor: Diane Ashmore
Production/DTP Editor: Steven Collins

Printed and bound in Spain by Graficas Cems, Navarra, Spain

All rights reserved. No part of this publication may be reproduced, stored in a retrieval system or transmitted, in any form or by any means, electronic, mechanical, recording or otherwise, in any part of the world, without prior permission of the publisher. Requests for permission should be made to the publisher at the above address.

Although every care has been taken in compiling this publication, and the contents are believed to be correct at the time of printing, Thomas Cook Tour Operations Limited cannot accept any responsibility for errors or omission, however caused, or for changes in details given in the guidebook, or for the consequences of any reliance on the information provided. Descriptions and assessments are based on the author's views and experiences when writing and do not necessarily represent those of Thomas Cook Tour Operations Limited.

CONTENTS

SYMBOLS KEY

The following is a key to the symbols used throughout this book:

i information office	**✝** church	**☕** café
🚌 bus stop	**↘** tip	**🍸** bar
✉ post office	**🛍** shopping	**◉** fine dining
🛡 police station	**🍴** restaurant	

---

t telephone **f** fax **e** email **w** website address

a address **⏱** opening times **!** important

€ budget price **€€** mid-range price **€€€** most expensive

★ special interest ★★ see if passing ★★★ top attraction

MEDITERRANEAN SEA

CALA MORELL

La Vall

• Santa Àgueda

CALA'N FORCAT

CALA'N
BRUCH

CIUTADELLA

FERRERIES

CALA SANTANDRÍA

CALA BLANCA

CALA GALDANA

CALA'N BOSCH

EL LAGO

Cap D'Artrutx

MEDITERRANEAN SEA

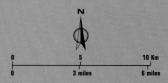

0		5		10 Km
0		3 miles		6 miles

◔ Cova d'En Xoroi, near Cala'n Porter

Getting to know Menorca

Azure skies, endless sunshine and beaches of pale golden sand washed by
a turquoise sea – Menorca has all the ingredients for a relaxing holiday.
Its beaches are some of the finest in Europe, from fun-packed family
resorts to secret pine-fringed coves. Its calm, clear waters are perfect
for swimming and snorkelling, or for learning to windsurf and sail. The
peaceful countryside of rolling hills, meadows and dry-stone walls forms
a gentle backdrop to the rocky coast, and the main towns at either end
of the island are an intriguing mix of history, culture and style.

SERENE & GENTLE ISLE

Each of Spain's Balearic Islands has its own personality. Menorca – also spelt Minorca – has often lived in the shadow of its larger neighbour, Mallorca, but it is quite happy to be known as the quieter and more relaxed of the two. It has little of the hectic nightlife of Ibiza, though there is plenty of fun to be had after dark for those who seek it. Menorca's character is different – serene, courteous, gentle, just right for a family holiday.

Above all, Menorca is a place to unwind, to eat the freshest seafood while listening to the sound of the waves, to walk across a herb-scented headland to find that hidden beach, to watch the sun set over the sea and enjoy the smiles on the faces of your children, enchanted by the magic of it all.

A LITTLE HISTORY

Menorca's history goes back a long way – to the Talaiotic period of around 2000BC. Not much is known of the island's early inhabitants, but they left behind a wealth of prehistoric monuments, from watch-towers to burial caves. Later invaders left their mark too – the Romans introduced Christianity to the island and established a city at Maó, the Arabs introduced horses, still a Menorcan passion, and the Catalan conquest of 1287 opened the way for Menorca to become a part of modern Spain.

THE BALEARICS

Menorca is the second largest of the Balearic islands, a group of islands off the east coast of Spain in the western Mediterranean. Mallorca is just 34 km (21 miles) away and the nearest city on the Spanish mainland is Barcelona, 225 km (140 miles) to the north west. Menorca lies about half-way between Marseilles, in the south of France, and Algeria, which is on the north coast of Africa.

⬛ *The splendour of the whitewashed town of Ferreries*

THE BRITISH CONNECTION

Menorca was ruled by the British for 70 years during the 18th century and the British influence on the island remains strong. It was the British who introduced Friesian cattle and helped to develop the dairy industry, which is still so important today. The first British governor built a road across the island, moved the capital to Maó, planted orchards and introduced new breeds of sheep and poultry. Several words in the Menorcan dialect derive from English – such as *mervils* (marbles) and *boinder* (which means a bow window, as seen in the old Georgian houses in Maó).

THE TWO CITIES

Maó and Ciutadella may be only 48 km (30 miles) apart but they face in different directions, as if they were deliberately turning their backs on one another. Maó, the modern capital, is a bustling city of businesses and government offices, with an old town of stylish shopping streets and one of the world's great harbours. Ciutadella, at the other end of the island, is much more traditional, with a Gothic cathedral and the palaces of the Catalan nobility, who refused to leave the city when the capital was moved to Maó. As a result, Ciutadella is the most Spanish place on Menorca.

The best of Menorca

SECLUDED COVES

Menorca has some 216 km (134 miles) of coastline with many small coves as well as the larger beaches. Most of these smaller coves can be reached either on foot or along farm tracks, after paying a small entrance fee when crossing private land. They are often pine-fringed, with beautiful clear water, although they have no facilities. Nevertheless, they are very popular with the local people and are extremely busy at weekends. Try Arenal de Son Saura and Cala'n Turqueta, both reached across farmland south of Ciutadella (see page 86), or Cala Pregonda, on the north coast near Fornells (see page 62) – or take a boat trip from Cala Galdana (see page 50) or Cala'n Bosch (see page 54) to visit the many unspoiled beaches along the south coast.

BEACHES

Take a ride on a pedalo, swim in the sea or just lie on the beach soaking up the sun. Here are some of Menorca's best beaches, with facilities for all the family:

- **South coast** Punta Prima and Binibeca (see pages 29 and 32), Cala'n Porter (see page 36), Son Bou (see page 42), Sant Tomàs (see page 46) and Cala Galdana (see page 50).

- **West coast** Sa Caleta/Cala Santandría and Cala'n Bosch/Son Xoriguer (see page 54).

- **North coast** Arenal d'en Castell and Son Parc (page 66), and Fornells/ Cala Tirant (see page 62).

BEST OF THE REST

- Wander the back streets of Maó (see page 14), Ferreries (see page 80) and Ciutadella (see page 86), browsing in small, specialist shops among the hidden alleyways.

- Visit Maó's market (see page 19) to taste some Mahón cheese, take a boat tour around Maó harbour (see page 22), then look into the Xoriguer distillery on the waterfront to sample the local *pomada* (gin with lemon).

- Visit Monte Toro (see page 77), Menorca's highest point.

- Try *caldereta de langosta* (lobster casserole) beside the harbour at Fornells (see page 62).

- Have lunch in Ciutadella harbour (see page 86) beneath the old city walls.

- Go to the trotting races (see page 108) in Maó and Ciutadella at weekends – and have a flutter.

- Learn about Menorca's history – complete with sound effects – at Fort Marlborough (see page 23) near Es Castell.

- See the whitewashed 'fishing village' at Binibeca Vell (see page 32).

- Seek out some of Menorca's ancient monuments, such as the Naveta d'es Tudons burial chamber near Ciutadella (see page 88).

- Watch the sun go down on the west coast (see pages 54 and 77), with Mallorca silhouetted on the horizon... then watch the moon come up from the Xoroi caves in Cala'n Porter (see page 36).

RESORTS
Places under the sun

Maó
stately Georgian capital

Founded in Roman times and rebuilt after the Catalan conquest, the city of Maó – also known as Mahón – reached its heyday when the first British governor, Sir Richard Kane, moved the capital here from Ciutadella in 1722. You can still feel the British influence today, in streets like Carrer Isabel II, whose fine Georgian houses feature sash windows.

Maó (pronounced 'Ma-oh') is a city for strolling, especially along the pedestrian shopping streets which tumble down the hill from the main square, **Plaça de S'Esplanada**, to the port. Wander down any side streets and you come across hidden alleys, stylish shops or an unexpected glimpse of an ancient archway, the only surviving section of the old city walls.

Plaça de S'Esplanada is the city's meeting place, where children play and old men sit beneath the trees while the bustling life of a modern capital goes on around them – the best place to watch it all happening is from one of the cafés lining the square.

THINGS TO SEE & DO
Local museums ★

Ateneu is Maó's natural history museum, with magnificent cabinets of stuffed seabirds, spiny crabs and lobsters, and fossils (🅐 Carrer de Cifuentes 25 ☎ 971 36 05 53 🕒 Open Mon–Fri 10.00–1.00 and 16.00–20.00, Sat 16.00–20.00). **Museu Hernández Mora** has a fascinating collection of island maps bequeathed by a local author (🅐 Claustre del Carme ☎ 971 35 05 97 🌐 www.ajmao.org 🕒 Open Mon–Sat 10.00–13.00).

DID YOU KNOW?
Maó, or Mahón as it is often called, gave mayonnaise to the world. The word was invented by the French Duke of Richelieu, who used it as an aphrodisiac – *mahonesa* translates as 'a girl from Mahón'!

▲ *Beneath the city walls in Maó*

Museu de Menorca ★★★
This museum, in the cloisters of the former Franciscan convent, contains finds from the many Bronze Age sites that have been discovered on Menorca. ⓐ Plaça d'es Monestir ⏱ Open Tues–Sat 10.00–14.00 and 17.00–20.00, Sun 10.00–14.00, closed Mon (Apr–Sept); Tues–Sat 10.00–13.00 and 16.00–18.00, Sun 10.00–14.00, closed Mon (Oct–Mar)

Santa Maria ★
The highlight of Maó's biggest church is its Swiss organ, with more than 3000 pipes. Organ concerts are given from July to September at 11.00 every morning except Sundays. ⏱ Open 08.00–13.00 and 18.00–20.30

Teatro Principal (Principal Theatre) ★★
There is a variety of concerts, particularly operas, organised throughout the season. These are advertised in the local press. ⓐ Costa d'en Deia 40 ☎ 971 35 57 76

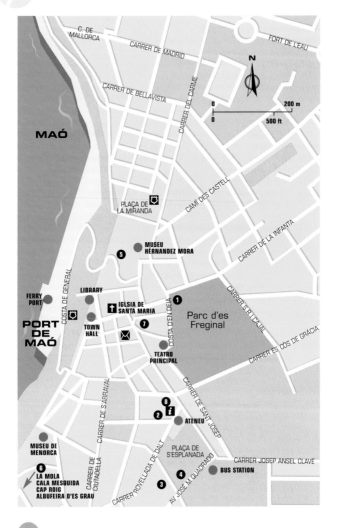

▲ *Maó's tranquil back streets*

EXCURSION
Albufera d'es Grau ★★

This beautiful natural park, centred around a massive lagoon about halfway between Arenal d'en Castell and Maó, is a paradise for walkers, bird-watchers and nature-lovers. Look out for such species as the tree frog, the ruin lizard, the aquatic terrapin, the booted eagle and the brightly coloured bee-eater. The long, sandy beach at Es Grau is ideal for children, with clear, shallow water and boat excursions to the Illa d'en Colom, Menorca's largest offshore island, named after a notorious pirate.

It is almost impossible to find a parking space in the city centre – your best bet is to arrive by bus, or failing that, drive down to the harbour where there is usually a little more space; or use the underground car parks below Plaça de S'Esplanada and Plaça de la Miranda in the centre of town.

RESTAURANTS & BARS (see map on page 16)

Most of Maó's best restaurants are down by the waterfront on the road around the harbour. Here is a selection of eating places in the city centre.

American Bar € **❶** A pleasant place to watch the world go by. The square outside is a popular meeting place. ⓐ Plaça Reial 1 ❶ 971 36 31 83 ⓛ Open 07.00–22.00

Andaira €€€ **❷** More like eating in a private home than a restaurant – top-quality Mediterranean cooking in a back-street house with a garden terrace. Expensive, but special. Booking advised. ⓐ Carrer des Forn 61 ❶ 971 36 68 17 ⓛ Open Tues–Fri lunch and Wed–Sat dinner; dinner only, closed Sun (July); dinner every evening (Aug)

Casa Sexto Quinqhela €€ **❸** Charming, family-run restaurant and tapas bar with a wide choice of meat, fish and shellfish dishes. Also try the home-made Galician wine, served in traditional style in white pottery cups. ⓐ Carrer Vassallo 2–4 ❶ 971 36 84 07 ⓛ Open noon–16.00 and 20.00–midnight ⓦ www.casasexto.com

J & J Fish & Chips € **❹** Traditional English fish and chips to take away or eat on terrace. ⓐ Plaça de S'Esplanada ❶ 971 36 94 13 ⓛ Open Mon–Sat 11.00–16.00, Wed, Thurs and Fri 18.30–21.00

Mirador Café € **❺** This friendly café, overlooking the harbour, attracts a young crowd. Bar snacks include delicious filled rolls and unusual salads. ⓐ Plaça Espanya 2 ⓛ Open Mon–Sat 10.00–01.00

San José €€€ **❻** The specialities at this British farmhouse restaurant include crispy duck and a steamed steak-and-mushroom pudding, available at 24 hours' notice. Booking advised. ⓐ Just outside Maó on the road to Fornells ❶ 971 35 17 59 ⓔ sara-sanjose@terra.es ⓛ Open Mon–Sat from 19.00, Sun from 13.00

SHOPPING

 Llibreria Fundació A good bookshop for maps and books on Menorca, and copies of the local English-language magazine *Roqueta*. ❷ Carrer Hannover 14 ● Open 09.30–13.30 and 17.00–20.00, closed Sat afternoon and Sun

Local produce Try Vallès bakery at Carrer Hannover 19 for cakes, chocolates and giant *ensaimadas* (light, fluffy buns dusted with icing sugar), and the long-established El Turronero confectioners at Carrer Nou 22–26, for such delicious treats as nougat, sugared almonds and toffee, lemon and meringue-flavoured ice-creams and Es Forn on Carrer Sa Lluna 26 for typical Menorcan pastries.

Market Maó's covered market is beautifully situated in the cloisters of an old Carmelite church. This is a good place to pick up everything you need for an afternoon picnic on the beach, such as bread, fruit, almonds, Mahón cheese, cured ham and several varieties of Menorcan pork sausages. The fish market is in a separate building down the road. ● Open Mon–Sat, mornings only

The Old Town The streets between Plaça de S'Esplanada and the market are where you will find Maó's most stylish boutiques. For good leather bags and shoes, look out for Jaime Mascaro, Patricia and Looky in Carrer Ses Moreres; Marisa and Mark's in Carrer Hannover; and Pons Quintana and Torres in S'Arravaleta. Other shops include Mango, also in S'Arravaleta, for fashions, and a branch of the Body Shop in Carrer Nou.

Supermarkets There are various supermarkets on industrial estates in Maó and Sant Lluís. ● Open Mon–Sat 09.00–21.00, some open Sun 09.00–14.00

▲ *Maó's seafront avenue*

Ses Palmeras € ❼ Popular with locals and visitors alike and centrally situated ⓐ Plaça Colon 6 ❶ 971 36 47 17 ◷ Open Mon–Fri 07.00–20.00, Sat 08.00–15.00

La Tropical €€ ❽ There are only a few outdoor tables on a busy street, but this typical Spanish restaurant serves some of the best and freshest food in town. Try the 'menu from the market', which changes daily. ⓐ Carrer La Lluna 36 ❶ 971 36 05 56 ◷ Open 13.00–16.00 and 19.30–midnight

NIGHTLIFE

Maó's main nightlife district is down on the waterfront at Moll de Ponent, but there are also a few fashionable nightspots in the town centre:

Café Blues Trendy basement bar, playing mostly jazz and blues.
ⓐ Carrer Santiago Ramon i Cajal 3 🕐 Open Tues–Sun from 19.00

Si The only centrally located disco in town, popular with locals and tourists alike. ⓐ Carrer Verge de Gràcia 16 🕾 971 36 13 62
🕐 Open 23.30–03.00

Maó harbour & Es Castell
historic natural harbour

The harbour, which is 5 km (3 miles) long and 1 km (approx half a mile) wide at its widest point, is the second largest natural deep water port in the world after Pearl Harbour. Due to this fact, and its location in the Mediterranean, it has been a natural strategic stronghold for many nations throughout history. Today, its cruise ships, naval vessels, fishing boats and numerous luxury yachts can be viewed from one of the vantage points, such as Plaça de la Miranda.

The best way to see the harbour is to join one of the boat tours that leave regularly from both Maó and Es Castell. The guides point out the famous buildings lining the banks, such as **Golden Farm**, the plum-red Georgian mansion high on the northern shore, where Lord Nelson, the British admiral, is supposed to have stayed with Lady Hamilton, his mistress, and one of Richard Branson's holiday homes. Out in the harbour are three islands: the first, **Illa del Rei** ('King's Island'), is where Alfonso III landed in 1287 to capture Menorca from the Moors. The British later built a hospital here and renamed it 'Bloody Island'. Further out, watching over the harbour, is **La Mola**, a Spanish military base at the most easterly point in Spain.

On the other side of the harbour is the old British garrison town of **Es Castell**, the most easterly town in Spain. Also previously known as Villacarlos by the Spanish and Georgetown by the British, it contains many Georgian buildings – especially round the main square, Plaça de S'Esplanada. One of the former barracks contains an interesting **military**

SHOPPING

 There are several shops along the waterfront of Maó where you can buy a range of good ceramics and many other Menorcan souvenirs.

🔺 *Maó harbour has been strategically important throughout history*

museum (🅐 Plaça de S'Esplanada 🕒 Open Sat and Sun 11.00–13.00). The harbour at **Cales Fonts** here is perfectly placed to catch the afternoon sun and many people come here to eat at the numerous harbourside restaurants, both at lunchtime and in the evenings.

THINGS TO SEE & DO
Fort Marlborough ★★
This British-built 18th-century fortress, near the entrance to Maó harbour at picturesque Cala de Sant Esteve, has been restored and opened as a tourist attraction. Take the entrance in the centre of Sant Esteve. You can walk along underground tunnels still smelling of gunpowder, enjoying the special effects – including the odd explosion. ☎ 971 36 04 62
🕒 Open Tues–Sat 09.00–13.00 and 15.00–19.00, Sun 10.00–13.00
🛈 Admission charge

Cala Figuera

ES CASTELL

MOLL DE LLEVANT

PASSEIG MARITIM

CALLE DE CALA FIGUERA

AV PORT DE MAÓ

FORT DE L'EAU

C. DE MALLORCA

CARRER DE MADRID

MOLL DE LLEVANT

CARRER DE BELLAVISTA

MAÓ HARBOUR

CARRER DEL CARME

CAMÍ DES CASTELL

CARRER DE LA INFANTA

CARRER SANT LLUIS GONÇA

CARRER DE SANT MANUEL

COSTA DE GENERAL

CARRER S R I CAJAL

CARRER DE GRÀCIA

Parc d'es Freginal

CARRER ES COS DE GRÀCIA

C. SA SÍNIA COSTABELLA

AV DE FRANCESC FEMENIAS

1 **MUSEU HERNÁNDEZ MORA**

2 **LIBRARY**

3 **TOWN HALL**

4 **TEATRO PRINCIPAL**

5 **ATENEU**

6 **MUSEO DE MENORCA**

7 **XORIGUER**

CARRER DE SANT JOSEP

CARRER S'ARRAVAL

CARRER ROVELLADA DE DALT

PLAÇA DE S'ESPLANADA

CARRER JOSEP ANSEL CLAVÉ

CARRER DE PEDRO MARIA CARDONA

AV DE LA MEDITERRANEA

LA MOLA CALA MESQUIDA

CARRER DE CIUTADELLA

AV JOSE M QUADRADO

CARRER DE M LLUÏSA SERRA

AVINGUDA DE VIVES LLULL

300 m

1000 ft

Harbour tours ★★★

These leave frequently from Maó waterfront and from Cales Fonts in Es Castell. Some of the tours use glass-bottomed boats, allowing you to see deep beneath the water.

Xoriguer ★

Visit this gin distillery on the waterfront of Maó to see the old-fashioned copper stills and taste a wide range of gin-based liqueurs, which are famous on the island. ⓐ Andén de Poniente 91 ① 971 36 21 97 ⓦ www.xoriguer.es ① Open Mon–Fri 08.00–19.00, Sat 09.00–13.00

BEACHES

There are no beaches anywhere in Maó harbour. The nearest is at **Cala Mesquida**, signposted from the road between Maó and La Mola. The beach here, and the Es Cap Roig fish restaurant (specializing in *cap roig*, or fish scorpion, see page 26) on the cliffs, are popular weekend retreats for the people of Maó.

RESTAURANTS

The restaurants along the harbours both in Maó and Es Castell are all worth a visit depending on your taste and size of your pocket! There are a variety of gastronomical delights to be tried from local Menorcan cuisine to Italian, Indian and Chinese; serving anything from a snack to a 5- or 6-course speciality. The following are worthy of note.

 Although lunch in Spain does not usually start much before 14.00, arrive early to snap up one of the harbourside tables in Maó or Es Castell.

Maó (see map on page 24)

 Es Cap Roig €€€ ① Fish served in a dream setting on top of the slate cliffs at Cala Mesquida. Worth it for a special treat. ⓐ Cala Mesquida, on the way into the village ① 971 18 83 83 ① Open noon–16.00 and 19.00–midnight except Mon lunchtime ① Booking advised

La Minerva €€€ **②** Part floating restaurant, part converted warehouse, with top-notch dishes such as steak with *foie gras* and salmon with pink peppercorns. **ⓐ** Moll de Llevant 87 **ⓣ** 971 35 19 95 **ⓛ** Open noon–15.00 and 20.00–23.00

Roma €€ **③** Popular pizza and pasta restaurant beside the moorings. **ⓐ** Moll de Llevant 295 **ⓣ** 971 35 37 77. **ⓛ** Open 12.30–midnight

Es Castell (see map on page 27)

Bar España €€ **①** Extremely popular with the locals and visitors alike – try the soufflé sweet. Air-conditioned. **ⓐ** Carrer Victori 48–50 **ⓣ** 971 36 32 99 **ⓛ** Open 12.30–15.30 and 19.30–23.00

Ca'n Delio €€ **②** What could be more romantic than fresh sardines and chilled wine beside the sea on a summer evening? **ⓐ** Cales Fonts 38 **ⓣ** 971 35 17 11 **ⓛ** Open 12.30–15.30 and 19.00–midnight

NIGHTLIFE
Es Castell

Local musicians gather at **Es Cau**, a bar set inside a fishermen's cave in the tiny harbour of Cala Corb. For a more refined atmosphere, try the **Piano Bar** at Carrer Sant Ignasi 11 or Chéspir cocktail bar on the waterfront at Cales Font 47. The disco pub **Mamas and Papas** always attracts a lively late-night crowd with karaoke from 23.00–04.00.

Maó harbour

The area at the foot of the harbour steps from Maó is a busy late-night meeting place with several fashionable bars. Try **Akelarre**, **Pub Salsa**, **La Vaca**, **Tse Tse**, **Berry** or **Icaro**, which are all close together on Moll de Ponent and play a range of music. **Nashville** (€€ **ⓐ** Moll de Llevant 143), has German beer, food and live music some nights until 04.00. **Mambo**, (also **ⓐ** Moll de Llevant), is a highly popular late-night music bar.

MESTRAL

SANT LLUÍS
FORT MARLBOROUGH

GREGAL

LLEVANT

MIGJORN

TRAMONTANA

PINTOR VIVES

ME-2

Cales Fonts

LLEBEIG

PONENT

LLEVANT

MIRANDA DE CALES FONTS

2

● **HARBOUR TOURS**

CARRER DE SA FONT

CARRER DE SANT JOSEP

CARRER BELLA VISTA

CARRER D'ES PORT

CARRER ANGEL RUIZ / PABLO

CARRER SANT JAUME

CALA PADERA

DUC DE CRILLON

CARRER SANT IGNASI

CARRER D'SE CASTELL DE S.FELIP

PLAÇA DE
S'ESPLANADA

C/BATLE PONS

CARRER VICTORI

CARRER VICTORI

C. RELIGIO

● **TOWN HALL**

1 ● **MILITARY
MUSEUM**

MIRANDA DE CALA CORB

CARRER DE CALES FONS

C/ D'EN 'XISCO EL BARBARET'

Cala Corb

CARRER FABREGUES

CARRER CARLOS III

CARRER BON AIRE

CARRER SANT CRISTOFOL

CARRER SANTA BARBARA

CARRER STUART

CARRER GRAN

CARRER ANTONIA ORFILA

CARRER DE SANT JORDI

CARRER DEL ROSARI

CARRER DE MAO

ME-2

N

0   200 m
0   500 ft

● *Cala Alcaufar is the perfect spot to enjoy some peace and tranquillity*

S'Algar, Cala Alcaufar & Punta Prima
picturesque and peaceful

The stretch of rocky coastline running along Menorca's south-eastern shore is indented with pretty coves. There are few high-rise buildings and much of the area is still wild. This is where you will find some of Menorca's most peaceful and stylish resorts – including S'Algar, Cala Alcaufar and Punta Prima.

Punta Prima, at the island's south-eastern tip, was appropriately named Sandy Bay by the British during their domination of the island. The resort here has long been a popular holiday spot among Menorcans. Purpose-built S'Algar (pronounced 'Sal-gar') possesses some of the best sporting facilities on the island and a mini-train for the kids but, regrettably, no beach. Nearby Cala Alcaufar (pronounced 'Alco-far') is a tiny, relaxing resort, ideal for those who wish to enjoy the peace and tranquillity of rural Menorca.

Just inland from the coast is **Sant Lluís**, a dazzling village of white-washed houses founded by the French in 1756. In the surrounding countryside, you can still see some of the ancient farmhouses that once surrounded the village.

Not only is the S'Algar mini-train fun for children, but it provides a useful means of transport for adults too, with stops at all the key hotels, the S'Algar Sports complex, and the shops, bars and restaurants of the Commercial Centre.

THINGS TO SEE & DO
Hippódrome de Maó ★
Maó's racetrack is situated just outside Sant Lluís, and popular trotting races (see page 108) are held on Saturday evenings at around 18.00.
ⓐ Carretera Maó–Sant Lluís

Menorca Sports Centre ★

Offers bowling, tennis and golf practice. ⓐ Near Hotel San Luis in S'Algar
❶ 971 18 82 10 ◷ Open Mon, Wed and Sun at 10.00

Molí de Dalt ★

This blue and white windmill, at the entrance to Sant Lluís from Maó,
is now a museum with a collection of old farming tools. It is also an
information centre. ❶ 971 15 10 84 ◷ Open Mon–Fri 10.00–14.00 and
18.00–20.00, Sat 10.00–13.00, Sun 11.00–13.00

S'Algar Sports ★★

An extensive complex offering a wide range of sports from mountain
biking, sailing and kayaking to tennis, mini-golf, archery and bowls.
(ⓐ Club Hotel San Luís ❶ 971 35 94 54 ◷ Open 10.00–13.00). There's
also a daily Kids' Club (◷ Open 15.00–17.30). ❶ You need to reserve the
activities 24 hours beforehand at the Info-desk opposite La Raqueta café

Water sports ★★

Try your hand at diving, water-skiing or sailing. ⓐ Passeig Marítim,
S'Algar ❶ 971 15 06 10

BEACHES

The largest beach in south-eastern Menorca is at **Punta Prima**, looking
across to the tiny island of Isla de l'Aire, uninhabited except for a rare
species of black lizard. The lovely sandy beach which gently shelves into
the crystal-clear waters of the pretty, cliff-lined bay at **Cala Alcaufar**
makes it a popular choice for families and non-swimmers. Both beaches
have sunbeds and parasols for hire, and also pedalos at Punta Prima.

RESTAURANTS

Las Palmeras €€ This popular pizzeria-grill restaurant is part
of the Las Palmeras apartment complex. Children can swim
in the pool, while adults eat. ⓐ S'Algar ❶ 971 15 06 03
ⓦ www.salgarhotels.com ◷ Open 13.00–15.30 and 19.00–23.00

Pan y Vino €€€ Stylish British-run restaurant in a 200-year-old farmhouse in the charming hamlet of Torret, between Punta Prima and Sant Lluís. Booking is essential. ⓐ Camí de la Coixa 3, Torret ❶ 971 15 03 22 ⏰ Open 20.00–23.00

La Rueda €€ Busy village restaurant (upstairs) and tapas bar on the main street of Sant Lluís. The locals come here to eat fried squid rings, Galician octopus and meatballs in tomato sauce. ⓐ Carrer Sant Lluís 30, Sant Lluís ❶ 971 15 03 49 ⏰ Restaurant open 12.30–15.30 and 19.30–23.30; bar 06.30–midnight or later

⬤ Moli de Dalt

Sebastian Place € Popular bar and restaurant next to the beach with satellite TV and live music most nights. ⓐ C/Mayor, Punta Prima ❶ 971 15 90 68 ⏰ Open 10.00–02.00

La Venta €€€ Excellent restaurant opposite the roundabout, with ample parking across road. ⓐ Avinguda Sa Pau 158, Sant Lluís ❶ 971 15 09 95 ⏰ Open 12.30–16.00 and 19.00–midnight, closed Mon

NIGHTLIFE
Both the S'Algar Hotel and the Club Hotel San Luis in S'Algar have discos.

Binibeca Vell
award-winning architecture

The rocky coast from Binibeca to Es Canutells boasts some of Menorca's finest seascapes with its numerous small, sandy beaches lined with attractive holiday developments. The star attraction is undoubtedly Binibeca Vell, with an award-winning, Moorish-style complex designed as a modern fishing village.

The 'fishing village' of Binibeca Vell attracted international attention when it was designed by Antonio Sintes, the Spanish architect, in 1972. Until then, Menorca's tourist resorts had consisted mostly of high-rise hotels, but Binibeca was consciously different – a dazzling village of whitewashed cottages (even the roofs are painted white!) with wooden balconies lining a maze of narrow alleyways around a small fishing harbour. It has often been imitated, but never bettered, and Menorca's coastline is starting to look very different as a result of Sintes' inspired ideas.

Just a short walk along the coast to the east are the neighbouring resorts of **Binibeca Nou** and **Cala Torret**.

THINGS TO DO
Water sports ★★
The **Centro de Buceo** (diving centre) at Cala Torret runs courses in scuba diving as well as snorkelling tours by boat. ⓐ Cala Torret ⓞ 971 18 85 28

A road train runs to and from the resort of Punta Prima at regular intervals, stopping at key points along the way. It is particularly popular with children.

BEACHES
Binibeca beach, between Binibeca Vell and Cala Torret, has shallow water and clean sand, making it very popular with families. From the car park, a path leads through the pine trees to a shaded picnic area in the cove.

🔺 *El Pueblo de Pescadores, the fishing village, Binibeca Vell*

RESTAURANTS

🍴 **Bini Grill** €€ Family restaurant on the main square of the 'fishing village', serving grills, steaks and fresh fish. ③ Binibeca Vell
① 971 15 05 94 🕐 Open 12.30–15.30 and 19.00–midnight

🍴 **Bini Inn** €€ This friendly restaurant serves classic Menorcan dishes, such as roast suckling pig and oven-baked fish, on a terrace with a swimming pool overlooking the sea. ③ Passeig Marítim, Binibeca Vell ① 971 15 00 61 🕐 Open 11.00–midnight

🍴 **Los Bucaneros** € This shack on Binibeca beach has probably the best setting of any restaurant in Menorca – the perfect place to eat fresh grilled fish just yards from the sea. 🕐 Open 10.30–20.00

🍴 **DP** €€ Busy restaurant with hearty portions of Spanish and English cooking on a covered terrace overlooking a pretty cove. ③ Cala Torret ① 971 15 10 37 🕐 Open 10.00–midnight

🍴 **Sa Musclera** € It's easy to while away the evening in this cosy tapas bar at the heart of Binibeca Vell. ③ Binibeca Vell 33/34
① 971 18 85 55 🕐 Open noon–17.00 and 19.30–02.00

Es Canutells

Following the coast road west from Binibeca you pass many rocky coves and small beaches like Binisafuller, Biniparratx and Binidali, all worth a visit. Es Canutells is now a mixture of private villas and a holiday complex. There is a good sandy beach situated at the mouth of a gorge, protected from the sea by high cliffs.

Just inland from Binibeca and Es Canutells is the charming market village of **San Clemente** with its unexpected English inns and an excellent music bar, famed throughout the island for its live jazz.

RESTAURANTS & BARS

Canutells-Playa € Feast on the freshest of fish, a salad, crêpe or omelette on the shaded terrace of this snack bar overlooking the beach. There's also a children's menu and a take-away service.
ⓐ Cala Canutells ⓣ 971 18 89 34 ⓛ Open 09.00–00.30

Casino de San Clemente € Popular village restaurant and tapas bar which doubles up as a music pub, with live jazz on Tuesdays (from 21.30), which attracts international musicians. Visitors are welcome to bring their own instruments to the jazz sessions.
ⓐ Carrer Sant Jaume 4, San Clemente ⓣ 971 15 34 18
ⓛ Open Thurs–Tues 06.30–late

Coach and Horses € Once inside this pub you could be in an English village. Sandwiches, snacks, hot meals and English beers are all served. ⓐ Carrer Sant Jaume 38, San Clemente ⓣ 971 15 33 34
ⓛ Open 11.00–16.00 and 19.00–23.00, closed Sun and Mon nights

Es Molí de Foc €€€ This up-market Spanish and French restaurant has a garden which is just right for a romantic candlelit dinner. The specialities include duck breast with strawberry sauce and three types of paella. ⓐ Carrer de Sant Llorenç 65, San

⬤ *There are many rocky coves on the coast road to Es Canutells*

Clemente ☎ 971 15 32 22 🌐 www.molidefoc.com 🕐 Open 13.30–16.00 and 20.00–23.00, closed Sun night and Mon ❶ Booking advised

🍴 **Musupta Cusi** €€ Traditional restaurant in a small, old Menorcan farmhouse with live music every night. ⓐ San Clemente ☎ 646 67 86 44 🕐 Open noon–16.00 and 19.30– midnight ❶ Booking advisable

Cala'n Porter
Menorca's first beach resort

The setting of Cala'n Porter is magnificent – tall, pine-studded cliffs to either side of a wide sandy beach, with a stream tumbling out of a limestone gorge to run across the beach into a crystal-clear sea. The cliffs on the east side are home to restaurants, shops and bars, while those on the west are still totally undeveloped.

The best views in Cala'n Porter are from the **Cova d'en Xoroi**, a natural cave in the cliff face which acts as a bar by day and a disco by night (see page 40). The cave is the setting for one of Menorca's most enduring folk legends. The story goes that Xoroi, a one-eared Moorish pirate, was shipwrecked at Cala'n Porter and hid inside this cave. One night, while searching for food at a nearby farm, he kidnapped a beautiful maiden. They lived together inside the cave for many years and she bore him three children, but one day Xoroi's footprints in the winter snow gave away his hiding place. To avoid capture, Xoroi and his son leapt into the sea, never to be seen again.

 A steep flight of steps connects the main street to the beach, but once you have gone down, you do not have to climb back up – you could always come up in the mini-train instead.

THINGS TO SEE
Cales Coves ★★
This pair of rocky coves just east of Cala'n Porter is best known for the many burial caves which were carved out of its rock in ancient times.

BEACHES
On the beach at **Cala'n Porter** you can hire sunbeds, parasols and pedalos and you'll find a handful of beachside restaurants and bars. From the eastern cliffs, near the Cova d'en Xoroi, a path leads to two small shingle beaches at **Cales Coves**, where there is good snorkelling and swimming.

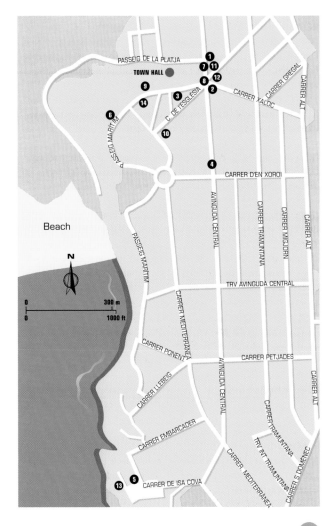

RESTAURANTS & BARS (see map on page 37)

Aloha €€ ❶ Every customer receives a garland in this Hawaiian-style cocktail bar on the edge of town. There is karaoke on Tuesday nights and a show every other Thursday and Sunday. ⓐ Carrer Xaloc ❸ 971 37 70 20 ⓑ Open 20.00 until late

Bar del Sur €€ ❷ A la carte restaurant that also serves tapas. ⓐ Avinguda Central 83 ❸ 971 37 71 62 ⓑ Open until late

Lorengo € ❸ Friendly family restaurant serving international cuisine with a Spanish twist. ⓐ Passeig Marítim 5 ❸ 971 37 71 96 ⓑ Open 10.00–16.00 and 18.30–23.30

Napoli € ❹ The pizzeria in the Siesta Mar apartment complex has live music three times a week. ⓐ Avinguda Central ❸ 971 37 74 11 ⓑ Open 09.00–11.00, 13.00–15.00 and 18.00–23.00

La Palette €€€ ❺ This seafood restaurant close to the Cova d'en Xoroi serves grilled prawns, peppers stuffed with fish and salmon in champagne sauce. ❸ 971 37 71 37 ⓑ Open noon–23.30

El Patio € ❻ Friendly, Scottish-run restaurant serving good-value British food. The bar has satellite TV and nine English beers. ⓐ Passeig Marítim 4 ❸ 971 37 72 06 ⓑ Open 19.00–early hours

El Pulpo €€ ❼ The name of this restaurant means 'the octopus' and the speciality is seafood, served on a shady terrace beneath the palm trees. There is occasional live music. ⓐ Avinguda Central 347 ❸ 971 37 71 10 ⓑ Open noon–16.00 and 19.00–midnight

Sa Paissa €€ ❽ Popular family restaurant in the centre of the resort with an extensive menu of home-cooked food including a good choice of vegetarian dishes and a children's menu. It also has a swimming pool with sunbeds and evening entertainment.

SHOPPING

Ca N'Andreu This shop has a good selection of souvenirs, including pottery, jewellery, carved olive wood and Menorca T-shirts. ⓐ Carrer Xaloc 3 ⓛ Open 10.00–13.30 and 17.00–21.00

Spar This centrally located supermarket stocks everything from Heinz baked beans and English newspapers to blow-up whales. ⓐ Avinguda Central ⓛ Open Mon–Sat 08.00–21.00, Sun 08.00–14.00

ⓐ Avinguda Central ⓣ 971 37 73 89 ⓦ www.sapaissa.com ⓛ Open 09.00–23.30

La Salamandra €€ ❾ Family orientated restaurant, with swings for the children, on a large terrace just off the main street. The bar attached to the restaurant has a dance floor and DJ. ⓐ Passeig Marítim ⓣ 971 37 74 53 ⓛ Open noon–midnight (bar opens at 22.00)

Seagram's €€ ❿ Tired of paella and grilled sardines? Ring the changes with BBQ ribs, fajitas and deep-pan pizzas at this American-style 'eating and watering hole'. ⓐ Carrer Mediterraneo 13 ⓣ 971 37 73 59 ⓛ Open noon–midnight

Southern Fried Chicken € ⓫ Chicken, hamburgers, BBQ ribs, hot dogs and pizzas. Eat in or take-away. ⓐ Avinguda Central, Cala'n Porter – opposite Sa Paissa ⓛ Open noon–00.30

Village Pub € ⓬ A typical British pub, with entertainment evenings. It stays open all day, serving everything from full English breakfasts to good-value main meals such as shepherd's pie and toad-in-the-hole to eat in or take away. ⓐ Carrer Xaloc 24, at the top of Passeig Marítim ⓣ 971 37 71 29 ⓛ Open 08.30–23.30

● *Pick of the beaches – Cala'n Porter*

NIGHTLIFE

Cova d'en Xoroi ⑬   After nightfall this popular lookout spot (● Open
10.30–21.00 ❶ Admission charge payable) turns into a disco, with
everything from soul to rave music on a dance floor perched above the
sea. Cova d'en Xoroi is a really good place to watch the moon come up –

and maybe the sun too! ● Disco open 23.00 until dawn ● 971 37 72 36
ⓦ www.covadenxoroi.com ❶ Admission charge

Stop ⓮ Cocktail bar where the young and trendy hang out late at night
– loud music and a great sangría. ❸ Passeig Marítim ● Open 21.00–05.00

Son Bou
Menorca's longest beach

About 3 km (2 miles) of pale golden sand, between rocky headlands, make Son Bou the longest beach on Menorca. The eastern end of the beach, where the hotels and shops are found, is always busy – but, as you go west, the beach becomes wilder, backed by sand dunes and freshwater marshes, which support a large population of migrant birds.

The resort has all the facilities you need for a seaside holiday – beach bars hiring out sunbeds, shops selling buckets and spades, safe swimming, and opportunities for windsurfing and water-skiing. Behind the marshes is the Club San Jaime, an entertainment centre at the heart of a tourist village, with restaurants and bars, a water-slide for children and a disco at night (see below).

Visitors have been drawn to Son Bou for literally thousands of years, and the prehistoric remains on the beach and in the nearby countryside are fascinating reminders of Menorca's history. As you stumble across the ruins of ancient churches and watch-towers, it is interesting to wonder what the visitors in 2,000 years' time will make of today's apartments and beach bars.

Climb up to the cave houses in the cliffs above the prehistoric basilica for the best views along Son Bou beach. And don't forget to take your camera!

THINGS TO SEE & DO
Basilica Paleocristiana (Paleo-Christian basilica) ★★
The remains of this 5th-century church were discovered hidden in the sand in 1951 and are now enclosed by a low stone wall. You can walk right around the outside, peering in at the ancient stone pillars and the enormous baptismal font, carved from a single block of stone. The basilica is located at the eastern end of the beach, beneath two large hotels.

◆ The long golden beach of Son Bou

Club San Jaime ★

The winding water-chute here is one of the most thrilling on Menorca and children are guaranteed to want to go on it again and again. There is also an unusual wooden labyrinth, Amaze'n'Maze, whose interlocking patterns change weekly. Adults can eat, swim or relax in the beautifully landscaped gardens where views stretch over the marshes down to the sea. ⓐ In the Club San Jaime apartment complex ⓣ 971 37 27 87 ⓛ Open 10.00–22.00; waterslides open 10.00–17.00; maze 11.30–22.00

Torre d'en Gaumes ★★

This prehistoric settlement, dating from 1500 BC, is about 5 km (3 miles) outside Son Bou and reached from the main road to Alaior. A footpath leads right around the site, which includes three well-preserved *talaiots* (circular watch-towers), a broken *taula*, or altar, and an ingenious water collection system. The views are spectacular. At one time this 'village' was home to 1000 people and may have been the capital of Menorca.

BEACHES

Only one – but what a beach! As you head west from two big hotels, the beach becomes quieter and there are far fewer people wearing far fewer clothes. The western half of the beach is unofficially nudist. If you tire of **Son Bou**, a half-hour walk from the western end leads around the headland to another fine beach at **Sant Tomàs** (see page 46).

RESTAURANTS & BARS

Boni €€ The speciality is seafood at this old-world restaurant and pizzeria with wooden seats and a great view of the sea. Order the mixed seafood grill and you will have enough for two. ⓐ Centro Comercial ⓣ 971 37 22 77 ⓛ Open noon–midnight

Bou Hai € Hawaiian-style cocktail bar where some of the waiters wear roller-skates. The drinks menu includes fresh watermelon, pear and carrot juices as well as alcoholic cocktails. ⓐ Centro Comercial ⓣ 971 37 15 72 ⓛ Open 15.00–03.30

Cafeteria Club San Jaime € This cafeteria is near the swimming pool so is a good place to eat when your children have finished in the pool and water slide complex. ☎ 971 37 13 75 🕐 Open 10.00–23.00

Cafeteria Manolo €€ This comfortable, modern establishment serves paella, pizzas, ice-creams and snacks throughout the day. ⓐ Centro Comercial ☎ 971 37 13 75 🕐 Open 10.00–23.00

Casa Andres €€ Friendly local restaurant featuring omelettes, pasta, steaks and salads. ⓐ Centro Comercial ☎ 971 37 19 18 🕐 Open noon–midnight

Copacabana €€ Disco and cocktail bar, Son Bou. Wonderful views over the coast. ☎ 971 37 80 47 🕐 Open 17.00–03.00

Las Dunas € A good selection of international cuisine, such as prawn cocktail, spaghetti and roast lamb, at this friendly terrace restaurant close to the beach. ⓐ Centro Comercial ☎ 971 37 16 65 🕐 Open 09.00–midnight

Il Gondoliere €€€ Smart, popular pizzeria and Italian restaurant. ⓐ Urbanizacion San Jaime ☎ 971 37 20 00 🕐 Open 18.00–23.00

Son Bou €€ Salmon, steaks, sandwiches and a children's menu are served on a shady terrace in the resort's main shopping centre. ⓐ Centro Comercial ☎ 971 37 25 03 🕐 Open 10.00–midnight

NIGHTLIFE

Club San Jaime The disco inside the San Jaime apartment complex plays a wide range of music to appeal to all ages and tastes. 🕐 Open midnight–05.00 ❶ Admission charge

Son Bou This disco is lively on Thurs, Fri and Sat nights and showcases DJs. ⓐ Centro Comercial 🕐 Open 23.00–04.00 ❶ Admission charge

Sant Tomàs
dunes and pine woods

Sant Tomàs (Santo Tomas in Spanish) is the smallest and quietest of the main south coast resorts, reached by a beautiful drive through pine woods from the village of Es Migjorn Gran. Everything at Sant Tomàs is centred on a single main street, with apartments, shops and restaurants to either side and the beach just a short walk away between the sand dunes.

The attraction here is the superb beach, covered in soft white sand and perfect for swimming or sunbathing. But if it looks too good to be true, it is – a freak storm in 1989 removed all of the sand and what you lie on today has had to be imported.

Es Migjorn Gran, with its pastel-coloured cottages in a maze of narrow streets, is a good place to soak up the atmosphere of a rural Menorcan town. The main square, **Sa Plaça**, is lined with bars and cafés as well as the **parish church of St Christopher**. This simple cream and white church, with its bell tower topped by a cockerel, looks much more Greek than Spanish and the whole town has a classic Mediterranean feel.

The unspoiled beaches beyond **Bar Es Bruc** reach right up to the fields – but be warned: the second beach, **Binigaus**, is very popular with nudists.

THINGS TO DO
Pony Club ★
This farm, hidden in the pine woods behind Sant Tomàs, offers riding lessons and can hire out ponies for rides. Booking advised. ☎ 676 68 85 78 🕐 Open 10.00–noon and 17.00–19.00, closed Fri

BEACHES
The main beach at Sant Tomàs is one of the best on the island – you can hire sunbeds, parasols and pedalos here, and there are also a couple of

● *The white sandy beach and dunes at Sant Tomàs*

good bars. At the west end, beyond **Bar Es Bruc**, the beach becomes known as **Sant Adeodato**; beyond this, past the rocky island offshore, is **Binigaus Beach**, where swimming is not recommended because of the currents. From the other end of Sant Tomàs's beach you can walk to the beach at **Son Bou** (see page 42).

SHOPPING

Galería Migjorn Owned by the British watercolour artist Graham Byfield, this gallery has exhibitions of his work and that of other local artists. ⓐ Carrer Sant Llorenç 12, Es Migjorn Gran ❶ 971 37 03 64 ❷ Open Mon–Fri 10.00–13.00

RESTAURANTS & BARS

Bar Es Bruc € Beach bar with simple food, such as sausages and burgers, and wonderful views out to sea. ⓐ San Adeodato ❶ 971 37 04 88 ❷ Open 10.00–16.00 for food; 10.00–23.00 for drinks

Ca Na Pilar €€ The locals frequent this restaurant because of its imaginative Menorcan home cooking. Booking advised. ⓐ Carretera Es Mercadal, Es Migjorn Gran ❶ 971 37 02 12 ❷ Open 20.00–23.00

Chic €€ This tapas bar and restaurant with a pretty garden terrace, in the heart of Es Migjorn Gran, is popular with locals and visitors alike. Choose from a wide range of traditional appetizers. ⓐ Carrer Major 71, Es Migjorn Gran ❶ 971 37 01 29 ❷ Open Tues–Sun noon–15.00 and 19.30–23.00

Costa Sur €€€ This formal restaurant on the roof of Sant Tomàs's shopping centre is the place to come for that special night out. It serves classic Spanish dishes, such as salmon and roast lamb, in an elegant dining room or on the shady terrace. ⓐ Platja Sant Tomàs ❶ 971 37 03 26 ❷ Open 12.30–15.30 and 19.00–22.30

Las Dunas € Popular family restaurant, with pool tables, crazy golf, a children's disco at 20.30 and a show at 21.30. The food is mostly pizzas and pasta dishes. ⓐ Platja Sant Tomàs ❶ 971 37 03 70 ❷ Open 12.30–15.00 and 18.30–22.30

Niko's Bar € This open-air bar is Sant Tomàs's meeting place, where everyone gathers around the pool at night. Snacks such as chicken and chips available at lunchtime, but drinks only in the evening. ⓐ Mestral Apartments ⓣ 971 37 03 70 ⓛ Open 11.30–01.00

Es Pins €€ A romantic and special place – a fish restaurant overlooking the beach, with friendly service and fantastic views. Try the seafood paella. ⓐ Platja Sant Tomàs ⓣ 971 37 05 41 ⓛ Open 12.30–16.00 and 18.30–22.30

La Ribera €€ This friendly café near the Lord Nelson Hotel serves a breakfast buffet from 08.30 to 10.30 and generous portions of hearty Spanish dishes, such as rabbit with snails, for lunch. ⓐ Platja Sant Tomàs ⓛ Open 08.30–10.30, 12.30–15.30 and 18.30–22.30

S'Engolidor €€ This family-run restaurant on a garden terrace behind a small Menorcan townhouse only has a few tables, so booking is essential. The food is traditional Menorcan, and the views are superb. ⓐ Carrer Major 3, Es Migjorn Gran ⓣ 971 37 01 93 ⓛ Open Tues–Sun 19.30–22.30.

NIGHTLIFE

Admirals Pub This busy nightclub on the first floor of the Hotel Victoria Playa plays a mixture of gentle pop and rave music. In July and August it is packed out with teenagers but at other times it is popular with people of all ages. ⓐ Platja Sant Tomàs ⓣ 971 37 02 00 ⓛ Open 23.00–03.00

Malibu Hawaiian-style beach bar with straw roof and parasols, managed by the four-star Santo Tomàs Hotel. ⓐ Platja Sant Tomàs ⓛ Open 10.00–23.30

Victory Club This smart disco, decked out with portholes and prints of Nelson, attracts all ages and plays all the latest sounds. ⓐ Platja Sant Tomàs ⓣ 971 37 01 25 ⓛ Open Thurs only 22.30–03.00

Cala Galdana
queen of the coves

**Cala Galdana – also known as Santa Galdana – has been called the
'queen of Menorca's coves' and its setting is quite spectacular. A river
runs across the beach beside a horseshoe of golden sand, nestling
between tall limestone cliffs and pine trees reflected in the sea. Many
people think this is the most beautiful spot on Menorca's entire coast.**

Until recently there was not even a road here – but now Cala Galdana
has grown into a busy resort, with villas and apartments climbing up the
hillsides and enough facilities to keep everyone happy. The dramatic
scenery of the bay and the south coast can be viewed from vantage
points on the clifftops, while the wide beach, with its calm water and
gently shelving sand, is ideal for swimming. There are several beach bars,
a wide range of water sports, plus mini-golf and a water-slide for the

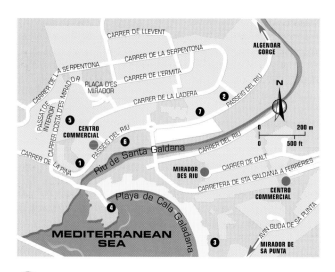

children. Cala Galdana is also a good base for gentle walks, to some of the quieter coves along this stretch of coastline, or inland between the walls of the **Algendar Gorge** (see below).

 An hour-long walk through pine-scented woods leads to the delightful cove of **Cala Macarella**. There's no need to take a picnic – the Café Susy is right on the beach and will even rent out parasols and sunbeds.

THINGS TO SEE & DO
Gorge visit ★★
A deep limestone gorge, **Algendar Gorge** has a marshy river running along its valley, that begins where the road runs out behind the Hotel Cala Galdana. Walk along the banks for wonderful views, especially at sunset. In spring and early summer the gorge buzzes with butterflies and birds and is covered with wild flowers.

Viewpoints ★★
Two lookout points above Cala Galdana both offer spectacular views. The **Mirador des Riu** looks down over the Algendar river and gorge, while the **Mirador de Sa Punta** gives sweeping views of the entire bay and right across the sea to Mallorca. Both miradors can be reached by car or by climbing the steep steps from the beach.

Water sports ★★
Motorboats, dinghies, windsurfing boards and snorkelling equipment can all be hired on the beach. Diving lessons are available from the **Submorena diving school**. ☎ 609 30 37 60 Ⓦ www.submorenadivers.de

The Cala Galdana Express mini-train is a fun way to explore – and it takes you to some spectacular viewpoints. ⏱ Departures every 45 minutes, 10.00–13.00 and 17.00–22.00

EXCURSIONS
Boat trips ★★
Glass-bottomed boats make regular trips along the south coast,
stopping at the beautiful Cala Trebalúger cove for swimming and
a picnic on the beach.

BEACHES
The beach at **Cala Galdana** has all that you could wish for, but there are
several quieter beaches that can be reached on foot.

East of Cala Galdana
A 20-minute walk from the eastern cliffs takes you to **Cala Mitjana**,
where adventurous swimmers can go right inside the limestone caves.
There are no beach facilities here. Cala Mitjana can also be reached by
car but you have to pay a toll for crossing private land.

West of Cala Galdana
The footpath from the Hotel Audax leads to **Cala Macarella**, where there
is a beach bar and several caves cut into the cliffs. Just over the headland
is the unspoiled cove of **Cala Macarelleta**, a lovely hide-away spot and
just 40 minutes' walk from Cala Galdana.

RESTAURANTS & BARS (see map on page 50)
Alexandra €€ ❶ This restaurant inside the Hotel Audax
serves top-quality Spanish cuisine, both buffet and à la carte.
There is usually some entertainment laid on during the evening, as
well as the Don Pepé bar. ⓐ Hotel Audax ☎ 971 15 46 46 ⏰ Open
19.30–22.00

Cala Galdana Playa € ❷ Friendly poolside bar inside an apartment complex, serving generous portions of Spanish food at very
reasonable prices – and with great views of the Algendar Gorge.
ⓐ Passeig del Riu ☎ 971 15 46 76 ⏰ Open 11.00–midnight or later

⬥ Cala Galdana beach has lots to offer

🍸 **Chiringuito Toni** € ❸ The best of the beach bars, in a quiet setting beneath the cliffs. A very romantic place to eat paella as you watch the sun set over the sea. ⓐ On the beach ❶ 971 15 46 32 🕒 Open 10.30–23.00

🍴 **El Mirador** €€ ❹ Seafood restaurant perched on a rocky outcrop overlooking the beach – from the *miradors* on the hillside you would think this was an island. ⓐ Over the footbridge from the Hotel Audax ❶ 971 15 45 03 🕒 Bar open 10.00–late; restaurant open noon–23.00

🍴 **El Rey del Jamón** €€ ❺ Typical Spanish bar-restaurant (the name means 'the King of Ham'), half-way up the hill behind the Hotel Audax. The paella is good here and the children's menu is excellent value. ⓐ Carrer Costa d'es Mirador 🕒 Open 11.30–late

🍴 **Tobogán** € ❻ This pizzeria beside the marina is a great place to take kids as it has a water-slide, playground and mini-golf course. ⓐ Platja Cala Galdana ❶ 971 15 46 16 🕒 Open 09.30–23.30

NIGHTLIFE

Mississippi ❼ Popular late-night venue with pool, satellite TV, cocktails and over 20 different beer types. ⓐ Passeig del Riu 🕒 Open 18.00–04.00

Cala'n Bosch, Cala Blanca & Cala Santandría
excellent base for water sports

These three resorts on Menorca's south-west coastline are very different in character. Cala Santandría is little more than a rocky cove, with a handful of restaurants and bars where the people of Ciutadella come at weekends. Cala'n Bosch – also known as Cala En Bosc – is western Menorca's water sports centre and a lively resort with two beaches and a wide choice of entertainment.

Life at Cala'n Bosch revolves around the marina, the starting point for a series of excursions along the unspoiled south coast (see below). The smart marina is lined with restaurants and bars where you can sit out of doors soaking up the sun and watching the yachts bob up and down in the water. Nearby Cala Blanca has suffered from excessive development but still has a charming pine-fringed cove lined with popular restaurants and bars. The main beach is just a short walk away.

Cala Santandría is linked to the smaller cove of **Sa Caleta,** whose beach is overlooked by an old watch-tower. This was the site of a French invasion of Menorca in 1756. Nowadays it is a peaceful spot with a sandy beach at the end of a long inlet and the only invaders are people looking for a place in the sun.

The cliffs beside the lighthouse at **Cap d'Artrutx**, close to Cala'n Bosch, are a great place to watch the sun set into the sea with the mountains of Mallorca silhouetted against the sky.

THINGS TO DO
Aquarock and Kartingrock ★★★
Fun for all the family. Swimming pools, slides, Jacuzzi, waves and games. Great karting track, single and double go-karts. ☎ 971 38 78 22
Ⓦ www.menorcaaquarock.com

⬥ *The Marina – focal point of Cala'n Bosch*

Diving ★
Accredited PADI training centre **Sub Menorca Diving Centre** ⓐ Hotel Son Falco Cala'n Bosch ⓣ 971 38 78 34 ⓦ www.submenorca.de

Water sports ★★
Sailing, windsurfing, canoeing, parasailing and water-skiing from Son Xoriguer beach, including special lessons for children. **Surf & Sail Menorca** ⓐ Water Sports Centre, Platja Son Xoriguer ⓣ 971 38 70 90 ⓦ www.surfsailmenorca.com

EXCURSIONS
Boat trips ★★
Various excursions are available from the marina, taking you along the south coast to swim at unspoiled beaches.

BEACHES
The beach at **Cala'n Bosch** is wide and sandy and deepens only gradually, making it safe for swimming. A ten-minute walk, or a ride on the mini-train, leads you to another beach at **Son Xoriguer**, where there are bars, shops and a water sports centre. The white sand and

safe, shallow water at **Cala Blanca** make this beach a popular choice for families. Strong swimmers can explore the sea-caves in the surrounding limestone cliffs. **Sa Caleta** has a sandy, small beach or you can walk around the cliffs to the slightly larger beach at **Cala Santandría**.

RESTAURANTS & BARS

The Britannia €€ This is a typically British pub serving meals. Large portions and a good variety of international cooking make this a must to visit. Satellite TV. ☎ 971 38 78 64 ⓦ www.britannia-elpescador.com 🕐 Open 10.30–03.00

Café Balear €€ Seafood restaurant beside the marina, serving everything from grilled lobster to squid in monkfish sauce. ⓐ Cala'n Bosch ☎ 608 74 48 16 🕐 Open 10.00–23.30, closed Mon

Es Caliu €€ Large, rustic restaurant on the main road; the speciality is charcoal grills. ⓐ Carretera Cala Blanca (near the turn-off for Cala Blanca) ☎ 971 38 01 65 🕐 Open 13.00–16.00 and 19.00–23.30

Ca'n Anglada €€ Friendly restaurant with a wide range of Menorcan specialities – try the special paella. ⓐ By the marina, Cala'n Bosch ☎ 971 38 14 02 🕐 Open noon–13.30 and 18.00–midnight

China Town € Menorca's original Cantonese restaurant. ⓐ Near the marina, Cala'n Bosch ☎ 971 38 57 06 🕐 Open 18.00–midnight

Cova Sa Nacra €€ This cool, shady cliffside bar and restaurant overlooks Cala Santandría. The restaurant serves tasty fish and meat dishes. ⓐ Cala Santandría ☎ 971 38 62 06 🕐 Open 10.30–midnight

Leli's € Family run snack bar/restaurant. Excellent value and quality. ⓐ Near the marina, Cala'n Bosch ☎ 971 38 73 90 🕐 Open 09.30–16.00 and 18.30–23.30

SHOPPING

 Centro Comercial, Cala'n Bosch The shopping centre at the north end of the marina has a supermarket, gift shops, a chemist and the Torres shop, selling handmade Menorcan leather shoes.

Hiper Ciutadella Out-of-town hypermarket on the road to Cala'n Bosch and Sa Caleta, just outside Ciutadella. ◐ Open Mon–Sat 09.00–21.00 and Sun 09.00–14.00

 Lord Nelson € Good food and a children's menu. ⓐ Sa Caleta Playa apartments ◑ 971 48 16 06 ◐ Open 08.00–midnight

Mirador Beach Club €€ Local cuisine overlooking the beach at Cala Blanca, with barbecues every evening and a swimming pool for the kids. ⓐ Cala Blanca ◑ 971 48 04 78 ◐ Open 09.00–03.00

Sa Quadra €€ Top-quality Menorcan cuisine at reasonable prices. Vegetarian and children's menus, and shady terrace. ⓐ Cala Santandría beach ◑ 971 48 09 59 ◐ Open noon–midnight

NIGHTLIFE

Big Apple Karaoke bar on the edge of Cala'n Bosch. ⓐ Carrer de Tramuntana ⓦ www.bar-apple.com ◐ Open 17.00–04.00; disco from midnight

Dreams Anything goes at this nightclub, which is popular with both locals and visitors. There are regularly changing theme nights through-out the week. Over-18s only. ⓐ Carrer de S'Abellarol 17, Cala Santandría ◐ Open 20.00–05.00 ❶ Admission charge

Moonlight It would be hard to find a more romantic venue for a cocktail bar; overlooks a tiny cove. ⓐ Avinguda Cala Blanca ◐ Open 10.00–03.00

Cala'n Bruch & Cala'n Forcat
fun for all the family

The rugged coastline to the west of Ciutadella is studded with rocky coves and fjord-like inlets of crystal-clear water. This area has grown rapidly in recent years to become one of Menorca's liveliest holiday centres, with a wide choice of restaurants, bars and nightlife. At the same time, just inland, you can still see the fields dotted with dry-stone sheep-shelters like pyramids.

There are four separate coves here – Cala'n Blanes, Cala'n Bruch (also known as Cala En Brut), Cala'n Forcat and Cales Piques – but over the years they have merged into one mega-resort, centred on the **Los Delfines** complex. Plaça d'Espanya, the square at the heart of Los Delfines, has shops, restaurants and even an open-air chapel. From here it is a short walk to any of the four beaches – and if you don't fancy the walk, you can always hop on the mini-train which tours the streets at regular intervals. These resorts make a great base for a fun-filled family holiday, with everything you need to keep people of all ages amused – and the city of **Ciutadella** is just a short bus ride away.

There are good sunset views from **El Patio** restaurant, and its neighbour **Es Bufador**, on the seafront promenade between Cala'n Forcat and Cales Piques.

THINGS TO DO
Aquapark ★★
Swimming pools with slides, crazy golf, open-air jacuzzis, playgrounds, mini-karting, bars and endless other attractions for all the family.
⊙ Avinguda de los Delfines ⊙ 971 38 82 51 ⊙ Open 10.30–18.30

Rent a bike ★★
A fun way to explore the resorts. **Velosplay** hire family-sized bikes by the hour. ⊙ Avinguda de los Delfines ⊙ Open 09.00–21.00

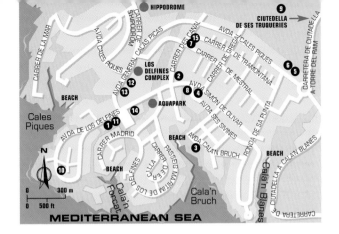

BEACHES

Each of the four coves has its own separate beach. The beach at **Cala'n Blanes** is long and sandy, with sunbeds, parasols and pedalos for hire and shady pinewoods behind the sand. **Cala'n Bruch** has very little sand, but the concrete platforms above the long, narrow creek are perfect for sunbathing or for diving into the clear water. **Cala'n Forcat** has a wide, sandy beach at the edge of a tiny cove, while **Cales Piques** has a small beach reached by a flight of steps.

RESTAURANTS & BARS (see map above)

El Abuelo €€ ❶ Everyone's welcome at 'the grandfather', where the good value menu features paella, grilled chicken and a mixed seafood grill. ⓐ Avinguda de los Delfines ❶ 971 38 81 54 ❶ Open 10.00–23.00

L'Ancora €€ ❷ This popular restaurant serves barbecued meat and fish on a shady garden terrace. ⓐ Avinguda Simón de Olivar, Cala'n Blanes ❶ 971 38 84 05 ❶ Open 09.30–midnight

Cala'n Bruch € ❸ Snack bar with a relaxed family atmosphere and wonderful sea views. Specialities include beef stroganoff and vegetarian lasagne. ⓐ Avinguda Cala'n Bruch ❶ Open 10.00–23.00

Ca'n Moll € **4** Menorcan fish dishes, such as grilled hake, rabbit in almond sauce and chicken with prawns, as well as a wide range of pizzas, served on a garden terrace. **ⓐ** Avinguda Simón de Olivar, Cala'n Blanes **ⓣ** 971 38 84 90 **ⓛ** Open 11.00–midnight

Churchill's Bar € **5** Good place to sit back and relax. Selection of food available. Bouncy castle, pool tables and games room. **ⓐ** Avinguda Cales Piques 225, Cala'n Blanes **ⓣ** 971 38 87 54 **ⓦ** www.churchillsbar.co.uk **ⓛ** Open 13.00–01.30

Hong Kong € **6** Buffet Chinese Restaurant. All you can eat for a set price; children's menu also available. **ⓐ** Avinguda Cales Piques 225, Cala'n Blanes **ⓣ** 971 38 84 23 **ⓛ** Open 17.30–midnight

Indiana Bill € **7** Menorca's answer to KFC, with an adjoining children's play area. **ⓐ** Carrer des Canal **ⓣ** 609 76 30 26 **ⓛ** Open 10.00–midnight

Lynne's Little Chippy € **8** Typical English-style fish'n'chips and snacks. **ⓐ** Avinguda Simón de Olivar 117 **ⓣ** 616 70 78 20 **ⓛ** Open noon–14.00 and 18.00–23.00

Mangiare Felici at Ses Truqueries €€€ **9** Italian and international cuisine in a country house setting. A very special place **ⓐ** On the road to Ciutadella **ⓣ** 971 35 91 59 **ⓛ** Open 13.00–15.30 and 20.00–midnight, closed Mon lunchtime

El Patio €€ **10** Seafood restaurant specialising in fish (especially lobster casserole), with marvellous views out to sea. **ⓐ** Avinguda de los Delfines **ⓣ** 919 18 48 64 **ⓛ** Open noon–15.30 and 18.30–23.00

Sa Caldereta €€ **11** Menorcan classics, such as lobster stew and roast shoulder of lamb, in a friendly family restaurant. **ⓐ** Avinguda de los Delfines **ⓣ** 971 38 82 12 **ⓛ** Open 11.00–midnight

🔺 *A fjord-like inlet at Cala'n Bruch*

NIGHTLIFE

Blue Breeze 🔟➁ Friendly, modern cocktail bar with pool tables and a happy hour 23.00–midnight. ➁ Avinguda General Calas Picas, Cales Piques ⓣ 971 38 81 53 🕒 Open 18.00–04.00

Cheers 🔟➂ This lively bar has karaoke until midnight followed by disco music till 04.00. Happy hour 23.00–midnight. ➁ Avinguda General Calas Picas, Cales Piques 🕒 Open 21.00–04.00

Danzas 🔟➃ Disco at the heart of the Los Delfines complex. Free entry for families until midnight; adults only after this. ➂ Avinguda de los Delfines 🕒 Open 20.00 until late

Green Parrot 🔟➄ Lots of fun and frolics at this English-run bar. Happy hour 21.00–22.00. ➂ Carrer des Canal, Cala'n Bruch 🕒 Open 19.00–04.00 (disco from midnight)

Fornells
peaceful fishing village

With its low whitewashed cottages, fishing boats bobbing in the breeze and stately palm trees guarding a seafront promenade, Fornells is everyone's idea of a Mediterranean fishing village. The fishermen still set out from Fornells each morning to catch the spiny lobsters which are the ingredient at the heart of Menorca's most famous dish – *caldereta de langosta*, **or lobster casserole.**

Fornells has its own beach resort – **Playa de Fornells** – 3 km (2 miles) out of town in the bay of **Cala Tirant**. The villas here are built in the local style and many of them have attractive gardens bursting with different varieties of cactus plants. Between here and the village is the water sports centre of **Ses Salines**.

But most visitors head straight for the village itself. Built on the west side of the Bay of Fornells, with its calm waters and long natural harbour, Fornells was originally founded to defend the north coast against pirate ships. Follow the waterfront beyond the fish restaurants around the main square and you come to the ruins of a 17th-century fortress, **Castell Sant Antoni**. Keep going and you soon reach the headland, buffeted by wind and waves, where a tiny chapel is built into the rock and you can walk right inside a restored watch-tower and imagine yourself on sentry duty looking out for enemy ships.

What brings people to Fornells is the chance to try the celebrated *caldereta*. The ingredients are simple: a lobster, some tomatoes and onions, a bit of garlic and parsley. It is all cooked in an earthenware bowl and served with wafers of dry bread to dip into the soup and a set of tools for prising the lobster apart. All the restaurants in Fornells serve it – yet each one is different and each chef jealously guards his own recipe. It is certainly expensive, but an experience to remember – King Juan Carlos of Spain regularly sails his yacht over from his Mallorcan holiday home to eat *caldereta de langosta* at his favourite restaurant, **Es Pla** (see page 65). How often do you get the chance to eat like a king?

⬤ *The attractive resort of Playa de Fornells in the bay of Cala Tirant*

THINGS TO DO
Scuba diving ★
Scuba-diving courses are offered at the **Diving Centre**, Fornells.
ⓐ Passeig Marítim 68 ⓣ 971 37 64 31 ⓦ www.divingfornells.com

Water sports ★★

The Bay of Fornells is ideal for novice sailors and windsurfers because of its calm waters and gentle breezes. **Windsurf Fornells**, at the entrance to the village, has dinghies, catamarans and windsurfing equipment for hire and can offer lessons for beginners and more advanced sailors.
ⓣ 971 37 64 00 ⓦ www.windsurf-fornells.de

EXCURSION

Cap de Cavallería ★★

From Fornells you can follow a narrow road to Menorca's northernmost point, the lighthouse at Cap de Cavallería, where wild goats graze on rocky headlands lashed by wind and waves. Along the way you pass the old Roman port of **Sanitja**, now a pretty harbour, with tracks leading to the unspoiled beaches of **Cavallería** and **Farragut**.

BEACHES

Playa de Fornells has its own small beach, with a footpath leading around the bay to the larger beach at **Cala Tirant**, where a beach bar rents out sunbeds, parasols and pedalos.

Fornells is a good starting point for excursions to some of the wilder north coast beaches, especially **Binimel-là** and its neighbour **Cala Pregonda**, which can only be reached on foot or by boat.

RESTAURANTS & BARS

🍴 **Es Cranc** €€ Where the locals choose to eat *caldereta de langosta* – no outdoor chairs and no sea views, just tremendous home cooking and a very Spanish atmosphere. ❸ Carrer Escoles 31
ⓣ 971 37 64 42 ⓛ Open 13.30–16.00 and 20.00–midnight

🍴 **Cranc Palut** €€ Quiet, out-of-the-way restaurant serving paella, meat dishes and fried squid, overlooking the bay at the end of the seafront promenade. ❸ Passeig Marítim 98 ⓣ 971 37 67 43
ⓛ Open 12.30–16.30 and 20.00–midnight, closed Tues.

La Palma/S'Algaret € These two tapas bars on the main square are always bustling with locals. **ⓐ** Plaza S'Algaret 3 & 7 **ⓣ** 971 37 66 34 (La Palma) or 971 37 66 66 (S'Algaret) **ⓛ** Both open 07.00–midnight

Es Passeig Marítim €€ This is better value than many of the waterfront restaurants – everything from pizzas and paella to a gourmet menu featuring octopus, mussels and lobster. **ⓐ** Passeig Marítim 45 **ⓣ** 971 37 63 12 **ⓛ** Open noon–15.00 and 1900–midnight

El Pescador €€€ Wicker chairs on the waterfront and a wide variety of fish and seafood dishes. Try red peppers stuffed with prawns. **ⓐ** Carrer de S'Algaret 3 **ⓣ** 971 37 65 38 **ⓛ** Open noon–midnight

Es Pla €€€ Imagine you're a king as you eat lobster at the water's edge. Some lesser mortals consider this restaurant rather too formal. **ⓐ** Avinguda Poeta Gumersindo Riera **ⓣ** 971 37 66 55 **ⓛ** Open 12.30–15.00 and 20.00–22.30

Es Port €€ Lobster casserole and grilled meat and fish are the specialities at this friendly waterfront restaurant. **ⓐ** Avinguda Poeta Gumersindo Riera 5 **ⓣ** 971 37 64 03 **ⓛ** Open noon–15.30 and 19.00–23.30

Rosa Negra € Hilltop snack bar and cocktails overlooking the beach. **ⓐ** Playa de Fornells **ⓣ** 971 37 67 16 **ⓛ** Open 20.00–late

S'Ancora €€ Popular fish restaurant facing the harbour. One of the set menus features a small tasting of *caldereta de langosta* at an affordable price. **ⓐ** Avinguda Poeta Gumersindo Riera 7 **ⓣ** 971 37 66 70 **ⓛ** Open noon–16.00 and 18.00–23.00

If you don't want to spend a fortune, you could try *caldereta de mariscos* – this seafood and fish casserole is the same as the *caldereta de langosta* but without the lobster.

Arenal d'en Castell & Son Parc
relaxing beach resorts

**The north-east coast between Fornells and Maó is the setting for two
of Menorca's biggest and best beaches, as well as a string of smaller
bays and coves. The coastline here is backed by sand dunes, with
acres of thick pine forest inland. The two big resorts have plenty of
restaurants and nightlife, but much of this area is quiet and unspoiled.**

The beach at Arenal d'en Castell is perfect – an oyster-shaped bay of
fine sand, protected from the harsh east wind by the headland of Punta
Grossa. Children can swim safely in the shallow water and facilities
range from beach bars to windsurfing. Nearby **Addaia** is a peaceful and
beautiful resort, set around a yacht marina at the entrance to a long,
sheltered creek. From Arenal d'en Castell you can walk along the coast to
Son Parc, another fine beach resort containing Menorca's only golf course.
Sa Roca, a few miles inland, consists of a few villas in the middle of
pinewoods, in the shadow of Menorca's highest mountain, **Monte Toro**.

 Don't forget to keep an eye on the safety flags while swimming
at Arenal d'en Castell (see page 115).

THINGS TO DO
Golf ★
Visitors are welcome to use the **Club Son Parc Golf**, a 14/15-hole course
(by reservation), along with the driving range, putting green and tennis
courts. Club hire available, but golfers are asked not to come in beach gear!
ⓐ On the road into Son Parc ⓣ 971 18 88 75 ⓦ www.clubsonparc.com

Hort de Llucaitx Park ★★★
Excellent facilities are available to dine, to hire horses and ponies, and
to entertain children at the playground or the animal farm. ⓐ Carretera
Maó-Fornells km 17 (near Son Parc turn-off) ⓣ 629 39 18 94 ⓞ Open all
year 10.00–19.00. Bar open all day; restaurant weekends only

● *The oyster-shaped bay of Arenal d'en Castell*

Water sports ✶

Both Son Parc and Arenal d'en Castell have facilities for windsurfing, and sailing dinghies can be hired from the marina in Addaia, where there is also the **Ulmo Diving Centre** (❶ 971 35 90 05 ● Open 09.00–18.00).

BEACHES

The beaches at **Arenal d'en Castell** and **Son Parc** have lots of facilities, are big enough to cope with large numbers and are suitable for families. A 20-minute walk from Son Parc is the pretty cove of **Cala Pudent**, where the beach is usually very quiet. There is no beach at Addaia, but the nearby village of **Na Macaret** has a small beach and several good restaurants.

RESTAURANTS

Alcalde €€ Classic Menorcan dishes, such as roast kid and fish stew, overlooking the beach at Arenal d'en Castell. ❸ Carrer Romani, Arenal d'en Castell ❶ 971 35 80 93 ● Open 11.00–23.00

Hallaissy €€ Serves fresh local produce. Specialities include chicken liver pâte and braised shoulder of lamb. ❸ Plaça Comercial, Son Parc ❶ 971 35 90 25 ● Open Tues–Sun 18.00–22.30

El Mirador € Pizzas and paella high above the beach at Arenal d'en Castell, with wonderful views from the shaded terrace and a swimming pool. ⓐ Carrer Estrella ⓣ 971 35 81 30 ⓛ Open noon–03.00

Puig de Sa Roca €€€ A special place for a celebration meal, this is a restaurant and swimming pool deep in the pine woods, serving traditional Spanish cuisine on a large terrace. Try the roast suckling pig or the cod with sultanas and spinach. ⓐ Sa Roca ⓣ 971 18 86 42 ⓛ Open noon–16.00 and 20.00–midnight ⓘ Booking advisable

Restaurante Addaia €€ *Flambés* are the house special at this popular Spanish restaurant. ⓐ Zona Comercial, Addaia ⓣ 971 35 92 61 ⓛ Open 11.00–23.00

Restaurante Son Saura del Nord €€€ The restaurant in the golf clubhouse at Son Parc has a Spanish chef offering high-class international cuisine. ⓣ 971 35 93 26 ⓛ Open 19.00–midnight, closed Mon. The bar is open 09.30–midnight

Rex's Pub € Homesick Brits gather at this typical English pub for hearty cooked breakfasts and snacks. ⓐ Zona Comercial, Son Parc ⓣ 971 35 91 05 ⓛ Open 08.00–18.00

S'Arenal €€ Restaurant and pizzeria on the beach at Arenal d'en Castell, live music every night. ⓣ 971 63 65 92 ⓛ Open 19.30–23.30

Tots Pub € Tapas bar popular with the locals, including the large British community in Son Parc. ⓐ Son Parc ⓛ Open 18.30–03.00

NIGHTLIFE

The Corner Bar This Irish pub has regular live entertainment and a large selection of Irish whiskeys. ⓐ Zona Comercial ⓣ 971 35 90 70 ⓛ Open 13.00–03.00 (karaoke Sun 21.00–01.00)

Alaior
Menorca's 'third capital'

Alaior (pronounced 'Allay-or') is sometimes referred to as Menorca's 'third capital', due to its historical role as a mediator between Maó and Ciutadella, and also because of the wealth and independence afforded it by its thriving leather and cheese industries.

Tourism has largely ignored the town and few visitors actually take the time to stop and explore the cool, shaded streets of Alaior, on a hill just off the main Maó to Ciutadella road. Those who do are richly rewarded by the striking architecture of its fine townhouses, the ornate **Town Hall** and the vast **church of Santa Eulàlia**. Be sure also to see the handicraft markets, the splendid views of the surrounding countryside from the water-tower and the striking **church of San Diego**, whose ancient cloisters have been converted into modern flats and whose courtyard, known as **Sa Lluna**, is a popular setting for concerts and folk-dancing.

Alaior's main claim to fame, however, is that it is the home of Admiral Nelson's favourite cheese, the island's renowned Mahón cheese, originally named after the port (Maó, also called Mahón) where it was first made and exported. Today, it is still made in the traditional way in Alaior, from recipes passed down from generation to generation. You can buy it in various stages of maturity from *fresco* (fresh and soft) to *anejo* (matured for two years, and as strong as parmesan). The more mature types travel well and make good presents.

August is the best time to visit Alaior, to see the popular **fiesta of Sant Llorenç**, flamboyant celebrations known in particular for their showy horse parades. Check with your holiday representative or at Maó's Tourist Office for exact dates.

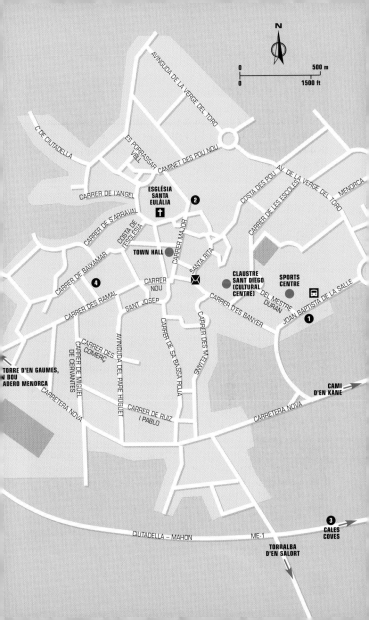

▲ *Alaior's narrow streets*

SHOPPING

There is a **night market** where ceramics, leather, cotton and silver are all on sale. There are also live demonstrations and workshops. ◐ Open Wed 19.00–23.00, June–Sept

For cheese, try the factory shops of **La Payesa** down an unlikely-looking back street (ⓐ Carrer d'es Banyer 64 ◐ Open Mon–Fri 09.00–13.00 and 16.00–19.00, closed Sat). Or try **Coinga** in the Industrial Estate on the edge of town (ⓐ Carrer d'es Mercadal ◐ Open Mon–Fri 09.00–13.00 and 16.30–20.30, Sat 09.00–13.30).

The main shopping street, Carrer des Ramal, has a selection of tempting stores including **Calzados Alaior** at no. 19 for shoes, and **Blanc i Verd** at no. 16 with its fine jewellery, pottery, wood and canvas gifts.

THINGS TO SEE & DO

Camí d'en Kane ★★

Menorca's first British governor, Sir Richard Kane, built a road across the island from Maó to Ciutadella – paid for by a tax on alcohol. The first section of the road (from Maó to Alaior) has recently been repaired and a drive along 'Kane's road' is a good way of experiencing the typical Menorcan countryside of cattle and flower-filled meadows. Turn left off the main road to Maó, following signs for the Camí d'en Kane.

Picadero Menorca ★

This popular ranch on the outskirts of Alaior offers pony treks, rides in a horse and cart, and special lessons for children. ⓐ Carretera Alaior–Son Bou (just off the roundabout beneath the Me-1) ☎ 608 32 35 66 ◐ Open 15.00–20.00

Prehistoric treasures ★★

The prehistoric remains near Alaior are worth exploring, particularly: **Cales Coves** is a necropolis (see page 36) that is an extraordinary

honeycomb of ancient burial caves gouged out of a cliff face.
Torralba d'en Salort boasts the island's most magnificent T-shaped
stone structure, called a *taula* (ⓐ Carretera Alaior–Cala'n Porter
🕙 Open 10.00–14.00 and 16.00–20.00).
Sa Torre d'en Gaumes is the largest prehistoric settlement on the island
(ⓐ Carretera Alaior–Son Bou 🕙 Open access).

BEACHES
The largest beach on the island is just 8 km (5 miles) drive away, at
Son Bou (see page 42).

RESTAURANTS & BARS (see map on page 71)

🍴 **Ca'n Jaumot** € ❶ A very popular local bar and restaurant.
ⓐ Joan Baptista de la Salle 6A 📞 971 37 82 94 🕙 Open
06.30–midnight

🥣 **The Cobblers** €€€ ❷ One of the best restaurants on the island,
in an elegant townhouse which was once the home of a famous
local shoemaker, hence the name. Most of the year, dinner is served
in the delightful courtyard. ⓐ Carrer San Macario 6 📞 971 37 14 00
🕙 Open Mon–Sat 19.00–23.00 ❗ Advance booking recommended

🍴 **Opera Due** €€ ❸ Typical Italian home cooking and pizzas.
Also pool and play area. ⓐ Calas Coves 📞 971 37 73 75
ⓦ www.operadue.com 🕙 Open 13.00–15.30 and 20.00–23.00 (May–Oct)

☕ **Transparent** € ❹ This trendy café bar in a spacious square
is popular with locals and visitors alike. There's a playground
opposite to keep children amused. ⓐ Plaça Ramal 22 📞 971 37 27 96
🕙 Open 11.00–02.00

---

❿ *One of Alaior's characterful courtyards*

Es Mercadal
Mediterranean market town

The picturesque old market town of Es Mercadal (pronounced 'Es Merk-a-dal'), at the geographical centre of the island, is known for its traditional crafts, its gastronomy, and the flamboyant displays of horsemanship during its dazzling July fiesta.

The name 'Mercadal' originates from the fact that the town was once the major market town of the island, where locals came to sell their fruit, vegetables and traditional wares, and to this day there remains a handicraft market, held on Tuesday and Saturday afternoons. Besides farming, the main industries here are the production of *abarcas* (sandals with soles made out of tyres), confectionery and almond macaroons.

THINGS TO SEE & DO
Explore the old town ★
As well as shopping on **Carrer Nou** (the main street) and lapping up the local colour of **Plaça Constitució** (the busy main square), be sure to explore the sleepy historic part of town, where whitewashed cottages straddle an ancient reservoir built on the orders of the first British governor, Sir Richard Kane.

Monte Toro ★★★
Es Mercadal is also the starting point for the ascent of Monte Toro, Menorca's highest mountain, named after a *toro* (wild bull) which, many years ago, led a party of nuns to a hidden cave containing a statue of the Madonna and Child. The active convent at the top has been a place of pilgrimage ever since. There is also a gift shop and café. The views from the terrace are sensational, especially at sunset. Most days you can see the entire island and, if the visibility is especially good, it is sometimes possible to see Mallorca.

◀ *Colourful displays of fans in Es Mercadal*

Sa Farinera ★★

The museum of the old flour mill, on the main road just outside Mercadal, with a commercial area (🕐 Open 10.00–21.00), a children's playground and a restaurant (🕐 Open 11.00–01.00). 📞 971 38 07 53 🌐 www.safarinera.com

Keep children amused in the car on the main road from Es Mercadal to Maó trying to spot a gigantic rock near the roadside shaped like the head of an Indian chief, known as **Sa Penya Cabeza del Indio** (Indian Head Peak). As you head towards Maó, it's on the right-hand side of the road (opposite a large lay-by) between Es Mercadal and Alaior.

BEACHES

Two of Menorca's finest beaches lie within easy reach of Es Mercadal on the north coast – **Binimel-là** with its striking red sand and pebbles, backed by sand dunes, and **Cala Pregonda**, with its unspoilt sandy beach and crystal-clear waters, a 30-minute walk along the coast from Binimel-là.

RESTAURANTS & BARS

Ca'n Aguedet €€€ Exquisite Menorcan cuisine and a good list of local wines. Try the snails with mayonnaise, then rabbit with figs, followed by a moreish dessert. The pinenut and raisin cake is particularly delicious. ② Carrer Lepanto 23 📞 971 37 53 91 🕐 Open 13.00–16.00 and 19.30–23.30

Ca'n Olga €€ Dine alfresco in a pretty garden, hidden down an alleyway in the old part of town. The cooking is Mediterranean style with some international dishes, and the *menú del día* is especially good value. ② Pont de Na Macarrana, Carrer d'es Sol 📞 971 37 54 59 🕐 Open Thurs–Sun lunchtime and evening, Wed evening only

Ets Arcs €€ Don't be put off by the exterior as there is a charming terrace at the back where you can enjoy generous portions of

SHOPPING

 Ca'n Pons This small, rather ordinary-looking bakery sells some of the best almond macaroons on the island. ⓐ Carrer Nou 13 ☎ 971 37 51 75 ⏱ Open 09.30–13.30 and 17.00–20.30

Ca's Sucrer An old-fashioned sweet shop, with jars of sweets neatly arranged on shelves around the store – an absolute must for those with a sweet tooth! ⓐ Plaça Constitucío 11 ☎ 971 37 51 75 ⏱ Open 09.30–13.30 and 17.00–20.30, closed Mon

Casa Servera Traditional *abarcas* (sandals) made on the premises. ⓐ Avinguda Metge Camps 3 ☎ 971 37 53 84 ⏱ Open 09.00–13.30 and 17.00–20.30, closed Sun

Galeria del Sol Affordable pottery and paintings of Menorca by local artists. ⓐ Carrer d'es Sol ☎ 971 37 51 25 ⏱ Open Mon–Sat 10.00–14.00 and 19.00–22.00, closed Sun

rabbit with garlic and other local dishes. ⓐ Carretera Maó–Ciutadella ☎ 971 37 55 38 ⏱ Open 13.00–midnight and 19.00–23.00

Jeni €€ A modern eaterie serving mouth-watering steaks, stuffed peppers and seafood. ⓐ Carrer Mirada del Toro 81 ☎ 971 37 50 59 ⓦ www.hostaljeni.com ⏱ Open 07.00–00.30

Molí d'es Racó €€ An atmospheric restaurant, in an old windmill, serving Menorcan specialities. ⓐ Carrer Vicario Fuxà 53 ☎ 971 37 53 92 ⓦ www.molidesraco.de ⏱ Open 13.00–16.00 and 19.00–23.00

Sa Plaça € A no-frills locals' bar in the main square, popular for morning coffee and tapas snacks. ⓐ Plaça Constitucío 2 ☎ 971 37 50 48 ⏱ Open 07.00–23.30

Ferreries
Menorca's highest town

Bustling Ferreries (pronounced 'Ferrer-ree-es') was once dependent entirely on agriculture and dairy farming. Nowadays, it has expanded and enjoys a thriving industry of shoe making, jewellery and furniture and is a popular shopping stop en route from Maó to Ciutadella.

The name of the town (from *ferreria*, the Catalan word for 'blacksmith') derives from its early reputation for making iron door hinges. The highest town on the island, it is also at the heart of Menorca's most fertile zone, and every Saturday morning there is a small market in **Plaça Espanya** where farmers from the surrounding area offer their produce of fruits, vegetables, cheeses, biscuits, honey, herbs and handicrafts.

Near by, the main square – **Plaça de l'Esglesia** – is one of the prettiest corners of town flanked by the small **church of San Bartomeu**, and the town hall with its brightly coloured flags. The narrow jumble of sun-baked back streets with their neatly shuttered, whitewashed houses has an air of typical Mediterranean tranquillity.

THINGS TO SEE & DO
Country manor house ★

The beautiful **Binisues** manor house provides a fascinating insight into aristocratic life in bygone days. There is also a first-class restaurant (see page 84) with magnificent views of central Menorca. ❸ Carretera Maó–Ciutadella, Km 31.6, then the turn-off to the right (signposted to Binisues) ❶ 971 37 37 28 ⏲ Open 11.00–19.00, closed Mon ❶ Admission charge

Hiking ★

The hour-long hike to the top of Mount Santa Agueda, one of Menorca's highest hills, is well worth the effort, not so much for the ruined Moorish fort of **Castell Santa Agueda** at the top, but for the breathtaking island vistas and for the incredible sense of history along the original Roman

road that forms a section of the walk. To find the start of the walk, continue up the same road as for Binisues and, just before the tarmac stops, there is a clearing on the right-hand side to leave your car, and wooden signs indicating the route.

Go-karting ★

Children of all ages love whizzing around the go-kart tracks at **Costa Nova Go Karting Club**. Two-person karts for parents with small children and karts for disabled people. ⓐ Carretera Maó–Ciutadella, Km 35 ⓣ 971 38 04 24 ⓛ Open 10.00–20.00 ⓘ Admission charge

Espectacle Ecuestre de Menorca ★★

Marvel at the equestrian skills of the **Club Escola Menorquina riding stables**, at their twice-weekly demonstrations of typically Menorcan dressage skills, including the prancing and controlled rearing often seen at island fiestas. ⓐ Carretera Cala Galdana, Km 0.5 ⓣ 971 15 50 59 ⓦ www.showmenorca ⓛ Shows Wed and Sun 20.30 (June–Sept). There are also shows 1 km (about half a mile) further along the same road on Tues and Thurs at 20.30

Museu de la Natura (Nature Museum) ★

A fascinating, interactive museum, which brings to life the history, culture and nature of the island. ⓐ Carrer Mallorca 2, Ferreries ⓣ 971 37 45 05. ⓦ www.gobmenorca.com/english/e_museum.htm ⓛ Open Tues–Sat 10.30–13.30 and 17.30–20.30 (May–Oct) ⓘ Admission charge

BEACHES

From Ferreries by car, you can easily reach the beautiful beaches of **Sant Tomàs** (see page 46), the neighbouring **Binigaus** beach (see page 47), **Cala Galdana** (see page 50) and near by **Cala Mitjana** (see page 52).

◀ *Horses play a significant part in Menorcan tradition*

SHOPPING

Castillo Menorca This shopping complex between Ferreries and Ciutadella is a great port of call for all the family – an excellent range of souvenirs in the shop and a pool, go-kart track and 4 acres of grass for kids (ⓐ Carretera Maó–Ciutadella, Km 35 ❶ 971 26 91 24 ⓦ www.castillomenorca.com). The huge **Lladró showroom** here has one of the largest collections of porcelain figurines in Europe.

Artesania Maria Janer You are sure to find some unusual presents from the large choice of quality pottery, wood, glass and paper gifts here. ⓐ Carrer De Sa Font 24 ❶ 971 37 40 02

Los Claveles This specialist bakery produces Menorcan biscuits and pastries. ⓐ Avinguda Verge del Toro 4 ❶ 971 37 31 28

Shoes are a good buy in Ferreries. Try the huge **Jaime Mascaro** factory outlet, the **Ferrerias Centre** and **Industrial Artesanas Menorca** factory shop on the industrial estate on the outskirts of town.

RESTAURANTS & BARS (see map on page 81)

Binisues €€€ ❶ A top-notch restaurant offering a wide range of meat and fish dishes. The proprietor has his own fishing boats at Ciutadella, so the house specialities include the freshest of fish, shellfish and lobster casserole. ⓐ Just off Carretera Maó–Ciutadella, at Km 31.6 ❶ 971 37 37 28 ◐ Open Mon–Sat 11.00–16.00 and 19.00–23.30

Liorna €€ ❷ This gem of a restaurant with a garden is hidden down a back street in the older part of town. ⓐ Carrer Econom Florit 9 ❶ 971 37 39 12 ⓦ www.liorna.com ◐ Open 19.00–23.00

Mesón Galicia € ❸ This is a small, homely restaurant and tapas bar which serves a range of hearty meat and fish dishes from

▲ *Pick up a bargain in Ferreries market*

Galicia, which is in northern Spain. ⓐ Carretera Maó 15 ⓣ 971 37 38 83
ⓛ Open Thurs–Sun 19.30–23.00, closed Mon–Wed

Mesón El Gallo €€ ❹ Try one of the specialities – *parrillada*
(mixed barbecue grill), steak with Mahón cheese or *paella de
Gallo* at this 200-year-old farmhouse restaurant. ⓐ Carretera Cala
Santa Galdana, km 1.5 ⓣ 971 37 30 39 ⓛ Open Tues–Sun 12.30–15.00
and 19.30–23.00

Vimpi € ❺ This no-frills locals' bar serves some of the best
tapas on the island. Try stuffed mushrooms, squid and local
cured ham. ⓐ Plaça del Princep Joan Carles 5 ⓣ 971 37 31 99
ⓛ Open 07.00–midnight

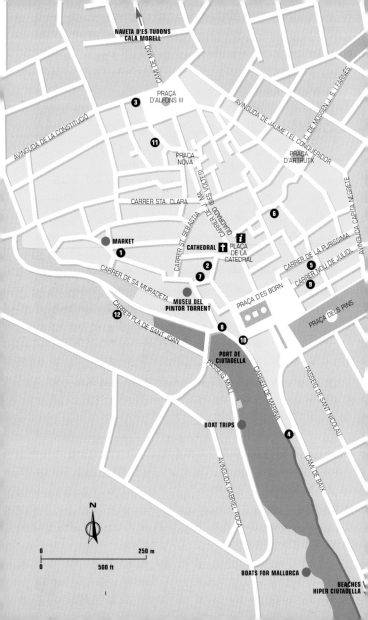

Ciutadella
Menorca's ancient capital

Nowhere else in Menorca feels quite so Spanish as Ciutadella (pronounced 'Suit-a-della') – also sometimes called Ciudadela, or 'little city'. When the British moved the capital to Maó, the bishop and noble families stayed behind, and their palaces can still be seen today. The Plaça d'es Born, the old parade ground at the heart of the city, is one of the finest squares in Spain.

In Ciutadella it is a pleasure just to stroll the narrow streets of the old town, located between '**the Born**' and the **Plaça de Ses Palmeres** ('Palm Tree Square'). Wander down any of these streets and you can peer into the courtyards of old mansions – with their balconies, stone archways and coats of arms above the doors. Artists and jewellers have set up their workshops in the back streets near the cathedral, among the up-market boutiques selling designer clothes. Come here in the early evening, as the people of Ciutadella gather beneath the whitewashed arches of **Ses Voltes** or stop for a drink at the bars in **Plaça Nova**, and you can really get the feel of this fascinating city.

Watch the sun go down behind the **Castell de Sant Nicolau**, an old watch-tower on the waterfront half-way along the Passeig Maritim. The views of Mallorca, as it turns pink on the horizon, are quite magical.

THINGS TO SEE & DO
Evening walk ★★★
The seafront promenade of **Carrer de Marina**, opened in 1997, is where the locals come to join in the sunset ritual of the *paseo*, or evening stroll. The full walk, from the **Plaça d'es Born** to the small beach at **Cala d'es Degollador**, takes a leisurely half an hour each way and the views along the seafront are superb.

Cathedral ★★

Menorca's Gothic cathedral was built on the site of a former mosque and the old minaret has been turned into a belfry. 🕐 Open 08.00–13.00 and 18.00–21.00

Museu del Pintor Torrent (Pintor Torrent Museum) ★

Art lovers will enjoy this small exhibition by Pintor Torrent. 📍 Carrer Sant Rafael 11 🌐 www.casamuseotorrent-menorca.com 🕐 Open 11.00–13.00 and 19.30–21.30

Burial chamber ★★

The **Naveta d'es Tudons** Bronze Age burial chamber in the shape of an upturned boat was restored to its original condition in 1975. You can crawl right inside on your hands and knees. 📍 On the main road from Ciutadella to Maó, 4 km (approx 2½ miles) from Ciutadella

Plaça d'es Born (Born Square) ★★★

The Born is the meeting place of Ciutadella and it is great fun to sit outside one of the pavement cafés watching the world go by. From the old city walls on the north side there is a good view of the fishing harbour at the end of a long, narrow creek.

EXCURSIONS

Cala Morell caves ★★

Just 8 km (5 miles) away on the largely deserted north-east coast of the island, this small, exclusive resort is best known for the prehistoric caves in the cliffs, which frame a picturesque cove and pocket-handkerchief-sized beach. The swimming and snorkelling are excellent here, just as they are at the idyllic, sandy beaches of Algaiarens near by.

Cruise the coast ★★

Take a day trip by boat from Ciutadella harbour to some of the island's most beautiful beaches, Cala Son Saura, Cala'n Turqueta and Cala Macarella. Most companies include free paella and sangría in the price.

⬥ *Ciutadella harbour is a good place to watch the sun set*

Hire a bike ★
Cycling is a great way to explore the city and the surrounding country-side. **Bicicletas Tolo** ❸ Carrer Sant Isidre 32 ❶ 971 38 15 76 ⬤ Open Mon–Fri 09.00–13.00 and 15.30–19.30, Sat 09.00–13.00, Sun 09.30–10.30

Mallorca ★★
Mallorca is just 75 minutes away from Ciutadella by fast boat, organised by **Cape Balear sailing company**. Between one and three daily sailings to Cala Ratjada, Mallorca (❸ Moll Comercial ❶ 971 81 86 68).

BEACHES
Ciutadella's beach is at **Cala d'es Degollador**, a short walk from the centre at the end of the Carrer de Marina. Most people head for the beaches at **Sa Caleta** and **Cala Santandría** or the rocky coves to the north of the city.

 *Ciutadella, Menorca's former capital*

RESTAURANTS & BARS (see map on page 86)

Bar Ulises € ❶ Join locals here for an early morning coffee in the market square. ⓐ Plaça de la Llibertat ❶ 971 38 00 31 ● Open Mon–Fri 06.00–15.30 and 18.00–22.00 (Fri 23.00), Sat 06.00–15.00

Café Central € ❷ A popular tapas bar beside the cathedral. ⓐ Plaça Catedral ❶ 971 48 22 08 ● Open 09.00–midnight

C'as Quinto € ❸ This tapas bar, specialising in seafood, is a Ciutadella institution. You can sit out of doors beneath the palm trees, enjoying grilled prawns, fried squid rings or the mussels known as 'sea dates'. ⓐ Avinguda de la Constitució 17 ❶ 971 38 10 02 ⏰ Open 07.00–late

Casa Manolo €€€ ❹ The best of the many seafood restaurants lining Ciutadella's harbour. The lobster casserole is expensive, but out of this world. ⓐ Carrer de Marina 117 ❶ 971 38 00 03 ⏰ Open 12.30–16.00 and 20.00–23.30

Don Giacomo €€ ❺ Pizzas from a wood-fired oven and imaginative Mediterranean dishes, such as duck with pears, served in an old townhouse close to the main square. ⓐ Carrer Nou de Juliol 5 ❶ 971 38 32 79 ⏰ Open noon–16.00 and 19.00–01.00

La Guitarra €€ ❻ Classic Menorcan cuisine at very reasonable prices in a basement cellar in the old town. ⓐ Carrer Nostra Senyora dels Dolors 1 ❶ 971 38 13 55 ⏰ Open 12.30–15.15 and 19.00–23.00, closed Sun

El Horno €€€ ❼ A sophisticated French restaurant. Try the rabbit with red wine and mushrooms, or chicken in cream and tarragon sauce. ⓐ Carrer d'es Forn ❶ 971 38 07 67 ⏰ Open 19.00–22.30

Marieta € ❽ This open-air waterfront café is always a hive of activity, and serves delicious sandwiches, salads and pancakes day and night. ⓐ Carrer de Marina ⏰ Open Mon–Sat 10.00–04.00, Sun 19.00–03.00

Pa Amb Oli € ❾ The place to try *pa amb oli* (see page 96), with baskets of garlic and tomatoes on the tables to rub on your toast. The other speciality is charcoal-grilled meat and vegetables. ⓐ Carrer Nou de Juliol ⏰ Open 09.00–midnight

SHOPPING

The narrow streets of the old quarter are full of small, specialist shops. Try **Carrer Seminari** for art, jewellery and antiques, **Carrer de Sa Carnisseria** for clothes, and the central street, usually known as Ses Voltes, for just about anything. Two good shoe shops in Ses Voltes are **Looky** and **Ca Sa Pollaca**, which has been selling handmade leather shoes since 1897. **Ses Industries**, in Carrer Santa Clara, has a good selection of Spanish wines and spirits. The colourful daily **market** in Plaça de la Llibertat is a fun place to shop for fish and foodstuffs. Also worth a visit are:

Hiper Ciutadella Out-of-town hypermarket. 🄰 On the road to Cala'n Bosch 🄻 Open Mon–Sat 09.00–21.00

The Magic House This toy shop promises hours of fun for children of all ages. 🄰 Carrer Major del Borne 7 ☎ 971 38 50 40 🄻 Open Mon–Sat 10.00–20.00

Sa Gelateria de Menorca This ice-cream company is famous throughout Spain and offers a dazzling choice of flavours. The orange and yoghurt ice is especially refreshing. 🄰 Costa d'es Moll 🄻 Open 11.00–midnight, closed Sun noon–14.00

NIGHTLIFE

Aladino ⑩ A trendy harbourside cocktail bar and dance club. 🄰 Carrer de Marina 🄻 Open 19.00–04.00

Asere ⑪ Salsa club with Cuban food, rum cocktails and great dance music. Go late. 🄰 Carrer de Curniola 23 🄻 Open Fri–Sun 19.30–04.00

Pla de Sant Joan ⑫ The open space behind the harbour is the setting for several late-night clubs and bars, mostly based in old warehouses. The best include **Lateral** discotheque and bars **Costa Este**, **Jazzbah** (live music) and **Ones**.

⬛ *Spanish fare – crayfish, fruit and white Sangria*

Food & drink

Restaurants in Menorca cater for a wide range of tastes – in the larger resorts you can get anything from an English breakfast to a Chinese take-away. Traditional Menorcan cuisine, however, is typically Mediterranean, making full use of local products – especially seafood – and heavily flavoured with garlic, tomatoes and herbs.

FISH & SEAFOOD

Local fish and seafood are always excellent – prawns and mussels feature on almost every menu, and squid, swordfish and sole are all widely available. Fish is sometimes baked in the oven with potatoes, tomatoes and breadcrumbs, but you can usually ask for it to be simply grilled. The most famous seafood dish of all is *caldereta de langosta*, a lobster casserole served in an earthenware bowl. You can eat this at restaurants all over the island, but the best place is definitely beside the harbour at Fornells (see page 62).

MEATS

The Menorcans are also hearty meat-eaters. Charcoal grills are a speciality, as are roast suckling pig and shoulder of lamb. Every bar has its own *jamón serrano*, a whole cured ham which is sliced into sandwiches or nibbled with pre-dinner drinks. The local *sobrasada* sausage, made by mincing raw pork with hot peppers, is delicious on toast.

TIPPING
Restaurant bills include a service charge by law, but it is usual to leave an extra tip of around 5–10 per cent for good service. In bars you usually pay for all drinks when you leave and the custom is to leave your small change behind.

PAELLA

The classic Spanish dish is *paella*, a mound of steaming rice flavoured with saffron and topped with everything from mussels and prawns to pieces of chicken. Paella is available everywhere in Menorca, but be wary of anyone who says they can serve you paella immediately – if cooked properly it takes at least 20 minutes to produce.

PIZZA

Pizza may not be a local dish, but the pizzas on Menorca are some of the best you will find anywhere. Most pizzerias cook them the Italian way, in a traditional wood-fired oven, with a thin, crisp base and toppings ranging from grilled vegetables to Mahón cheese.

TAPAS

These Spanish snacks are designed to whet the appetite before a meal, but order several portions and they can make an interesting meal in themselves. They are usually lined up beneath the bar in metal trays, so it is easy to pick out what you want and point to it. Typical tapas include tripe with onions, fried squid rings and meatballs in tomato sauce, but two of the best and simplest are *tortilla*, a cold potato omelette, and *pa amb oli*, toast rubbed with tomato and garlic and sprinkled with olive oil.

DESSERTS

Most restaurants offer fresh fruit or ice-cream – La Menorquina ice-creams, which originated in Alaior, are popular throughout Spain. An unusual local dessert is *crema catalana*, a custard with a caramelised sugar topping. If you don't have a sweet tooth, you can always ask for a plate of Mahón cheese, a strongly flavoured, hard cheese produced in Alaior (see page 70).

WINE & BEER

The best Spanish wines come from Rioja, though reds and whites from the Penedés region are often better value and Cava, or Spanish champagne, makes an inexpensive and special treat. Beer (*cerveza*) is usually lager, sold either bottled or draught – if you want draught, ask for *una caña*. Bars in the resorts have a wide selection of imported beers from Britain, Germany and elsewhere.

OTHER ALCOHOLIC DRINKS

Gin has been produced on Menorca for hundreds of years and the best comes from the Xoriguer distillery in Maó. You can drink it neat or with tonic, but the classic Menorcan drink, always drunk at festivals, is *pomada*, which is gin with lemon. Most bars have a good array of Spanish brandies on display. *Sangría* is an alcoholic fruit punch based on brandy, red wine and lemonade – delicious, but much more potent than it tastes. Try sangría made with champagne.

SOFT DRINKS

The tap water is safe to drink but most people prefer mineral water – *agua con gas* is sparkling, *agua sin gas* is still. Popular drinks, such as Coca Cola and lemonade, are available everywhere, and some bars offer freshly squeezed fruit juice or *granizado*, a fruit drink with crushed ice. The Spanish always ask for *café solo* after dinner – a small shot of strong, dark coffee, like an espresso – but visitors should have no trouble ordering a *café con leche,* made with hot milk, or a *descafeinado*, decaffeinated coffee.

EATING OUT

The Spanish tend to eat very late. In the larger resorts it should be possible to get a meal at any time of day, but in Maó, Ciutadella and the inland towns most restaurants do not open before 13.00 hours for lunch and 20.00 for dinner – and most people come a lot later than this.

At lunchtime, many restaurants offer a *menú del día* which is a set three-course meal, including wine or water, at a very good price. There is not usually a lot of choice but the food is always filling, local and fresh and makes a good option.

Don't be afraid to try local restaurants – most have English menus, and even if they do not, the waiter will usually be able to explain what's on the menu.

Menu decoder

aceitunas aliñadas Marinated olives

albóndigas en salsa Meatballs in (usually tomato) sauce

albóndigas de pescado Fish cakes

allioli Garlic-flavoured mayonnaise served as an accompaniment to just about anything – a rice dish, vegetables, shellfish – or as a dip for bread

bistek or biftek Beef steak; rare is *poco hecho*, *regular* is medium and *muy hecho* is well done

bocadillo Sandwich, usually made of French-style bread

caldereta Stew based on fish or lamb

caldo Soup or broth

carne Meat; *carne de cerdo* is pork; *carne de cordero* is lamb; *carne picada* is minced meat; *carne de ternera* is beef;

chorizo Cured, dry red-coloured sausage made from chopped pork, paprika, spices, herbs and garlic

churros Flour fritters cooked in spiral shapes in very hot fat and cut into strips, best dunked into hot chocolate

cordero asado Roast lamb flavoured with lemon and white wine

embutidos charcuteria Pork meat preparations including *jamón* (ham), *chorizo* (see above), *salchichones* (sausages) and *morcillas* (black pudding)

ensalada Salad – usually composed of lettuce, onion, tomato and olives

ensalada mixta As above, but with extra ingredients, such as boiled egg, tuna fish or asparagus

escabeche Sauce of fish, meat or vegetables cooked in wine and vinegar and left to go cold

estofado de buey Beef stew, made with carrots and turnips, or with potatoes

fiambre Any type of cold meat such as ham, *chorizo*, etc

flan Caramel custard, the national dessert of Spain

fritura A fry-up, as in *fritura de pescado* – different kinds of fried fish

gambas Prawns; *gambas a la plancha* are grilled, *gambas al ajillo* are fried with garlic and *gambas con gabardina* deep fried in batter

gazpacho andaluz Cold soup (originally from Andalucia) made from tomatoes, cucumbers, peppers, bread, garlic and olive oil

gazpacho manchego Hot dish made with meat (chicken or rabbit) and unleavened bread (not to be confused with *gazpacho andaluz*)

habas con jamón Broad beans fried with diced ham (sometimes with chopped hard boiled egg and parsley)

helado Ice cream

jamón Ham; *jamón serrano* and *jamón iberico* (far more expensive) are dry cured; cooked ham is *jamón de york*

langostinos a la plancha Large prawns grilled and served with vinaigrette or *allioli*; *langostinos a la marinera* are cooked in white wine

lenguado Sole, often served cooked with wine and mushrooms

mariscos Shellfish

menestra A dish of mixed vegetables cooked separately and combined before serving

menú del día Set menu for the day at a fixed price; it may or may not include bread, wine and a dessert, but it doesn't usually include coffee

paella Famous rice dish originally from Valencia but now made all over Spain; *paella valenciana* has chicken and rabbit; *paella de mariscos* is made with seafood; *paella mixta* combines meat and seafood

pan Bread; pan de molde is sliced white bread; wholemeal bread is *pan integral*

pincho moruno Pork kebab: spicy chunks of pork on a skewer

pisto Spanish version of ratatouille, made with tomato, peppers, onions, garlic, courgette and aubergines

pollo al ajillo Chicken fried with garlic; *pollo a la cerveza* is cooked in beer; *pollo al chilindrón* is cooked with peppers, tomatoes and onions

salpicón de mariscos Seafood salad

sopa de ajo Delicious warming winter garlic soup thickened with bread, usually with a poached egg floating in it

tarta helada Popular ice-cream cake served as dessert

ternasco asado Roast lamb flavoured with lemon and white wine

tortilla de patatas Classic omelette, also called *tortilla española*, made with potatoes that can be eaten hot or cold

zarzuela de pescado y mariscos Stew made with white fish and shellfish in a tomato, wine and saffron stock

Shopping

Every resort has at least one souvenir shop, but for the widest choice of local crafts you should wander around the old towns of Maó and Ciutadella or visit some of the factory shops strung out along the main road between the two. Es Plans, just outside Alaior, has a good selection of leather goods, pottery and jewellery, while Castillo Menorca, in a mock castle near Ferreries, has a Lladró porcelain shop as well as shoes, handbags, Mallorca pearls and lace. Llonga, in the industrial estate outside Ciutadella, has a wide choice of costume jewellery and leather goods.

Another good place for picking up bargains is at the weekly outdoor general markets which tour the island's main towns. The best are in the Plaça de S'Esplanada in Maó (Tues and Sat mornings) and the Plaça d'es Born in Ciutadella (Fri and Sat mornings). On Saturday mornings there is a craft and produce market in Ferreries. Other markets can be found at Es Castell (Mon and Wed), Sant Lluís (Mon and Wed), Alaior (Thurs), Es Mercadal (Sun), Es Migjorn Gran (Wed) and fresh produce markets every Mon–Sat morning in Maó and Ciutadella.

SHOES
Menorcan leather is wonderfully soft, and many of the shoes sold with Italian designer labels were actually produced in Menorca. Shop around and you can pick up some real bargains. Anything by Looky, Patricia, Torres, Pons Quintana or Jaime Mascaro is likely to be good quality. All these have their own shops in Maó and Ciutadella; also factory shops in Ferreries and Alaior on the main road Me-1. A Menorcan speciality is *abarcas*, traditional leather sandals made by stitching two pieces of cowhide onto a pneumatic sole. These are so popular that you can even buy pottery versions as souvenirs!

FOOD & DRINK
Mahón cheese, one of the best in Spain, makes a good souvenir to take home – it is sold in square loaves coated with yellow rind, and comes in

● *Browsing at a jewellery market stall*

several varieties, from young to very mature. Other good buys are almond biscuits, Spanish wine and brandy and Xoriguer gin, sold in earthenware bottles.

MAÓ AIRPORT

Don't worry if you've left your shopping to the last minute – the airport has good souvenir shops and a well-stocked tax-paid shop selling drinks, perfume and cigarettes. Visitors returning to other countries in the European Union can take unlimited perfume and wine, and any items bought in Menorcan shops – as long as you have kept the receipt to show that you have paid the tax. There is also a Jaime Mascaro shoe shop in the check-in hall.

Kids

Menorca is the perfect destination for a holiday with children. The locals adore children and will make a fuss of them wherever you go – even in the smartest restaurants. There are lots of child-friendly beaches, with safe, shallow water, Red Cross posts, beach toys and ice-creams for sale, and pedalos for hire. Most of the resorts have adventure playgrounds, sometimes with toboggan slopes and water-slides, and there are plenty of kids' clubs where your children can be looked after during the day while you relax without them. Your holiday representative will be able to give you more information.

Children love anything that moves. A boat tour around Maó harbour (see page 25) or a cruise along the south coast from Cala Galdana (see page 52) can become a real adventure with children on board. The same goes for a tour of one of the larger resorts on a mini-train – you can find these at Punta Prima, Cala'n Porter, Son Bou, Cala Caldana, Cala'n Bosch and Cala'n Bruch (see Resorts section pages 13–68).

Pony rides are available in Sant Tomàs (see page 46) or at **Picadero Menorca** (🅐 Just outside Alaior on the road to Son Bou 🕿 971 37 18 52). Another attraction for children is the equestrian show held at the **Club Escola Menorquina** which features carriage rides, horsemanship displays and donkey rides in the interval (🅐 Near Ferreries on the road to Cala Galdana 🕿 971 37 34 97 🕓 Show starts 20.00 Wed and Sun Jun–Sept). **Espectacle Ecuestre** also has horse displays (see page 83) (🅐 1 km (about half a mile) further on road to Cala Galdana 🕓 Shows Tues and Thurs).

Menorca's top children's attractions are the **Club San Jaime** at Son Bou – with a swimming pool, a water-slide and an interlocking maze, there is enough here to keep children happy for hours (see page 42); **Aquarock and Kartingrock** at Cala'n Bosch (see page 54) and **Aquapark** at Los Delfines (see page 58).

◀ *Capers in a canoe*

Sports & activities

Menorca is the perfect place for a relaxing holiday and for many people the most exercise they get is a walk to the beach followed by a quick swim in the sea – but if it's an active holiday you are after there are plenty of opportunities. The calm, clear waters of Menorca's sheltered coves make excellent conditions for water sports, while the gentle countryside inland is ideal for walking, cycling and horse riding.

HORSE RIDING

Pony and horse hire, as well as riding lessons, are available from the following centres:

Hort de Llucaitx Park ② Carrer Mao-Fornells Km 17 (near Son Parc turn-off), Es Mercadel ① 629 39 28 94

Picadero Binixica ③ On main road through Sant Climent ① 971 15 30 71

Finca Son Olivar Non ① 971 38 71 08

WALKING & CYCLING

Menorca Velo and **Menorca Trekking**, branches of **Club Activ** (① 971 37 38 43,) organise excursions into Menorca's hidden countryside. Bike hire is also available in the larger resorts. There are lots of lovely walks around the coastline to coves that cannot be reached by road – two of the best and easiest are from Cala Galdana to Cala Macarella and Son Parc to Cala Pudent. The Cami d'en Kane route is nearly 300 years old. From Maó to Es Mercadal, the 20 km (12 mile) historic trail can be covered by bike or foot, or even horse or car.

WATER SPORTS

Sailing and windsurfing schools include **Surf'n'Sail Menorca** at Son Xoriguer (① 971 38 70 90), **Windsurf Fornells** at the entrance to Fornells (① 971 18 81 50 ② wfornells@excellence.es) and **Sports Massanet** in Ciutadella harbour (① 971 48 21 86). All offer tuition to beginners and can also hire out equipment. The clear waters around Menorca's coves are ideal for snorkelling, but if you want to see more of the marine life and get inside some of the caves, you could try scuba diving. Courses for all are offered at **Ulmo** in Addaia (t 971 35 90 05 e ulmo@ulmodiving.com), **Sub Menorca** at Cala'n Bosch (t 971 38 78 34), **Cala Torret** near Binibeca (t 971 18 85 30), the **Diving Centre** in Fornells (t 971 37 64 31) and **S'Algar Diving and Aquasports** (t 971 15 06 01 w www.salgardiving.com). Remember that it is dangerous to fly within 24 hours of diving.

OTHER SPORTING ACTIVITIES

Bowls Visit **S'Algar Sports** complex (see page 30). t 971 35 94 54

Cricket The MCC (Menorca Cricket Club) has a grass pitch at Biniparrell near Sant Lluís. t 971 15 08 07 w www.menorcacc.com

Golf The 14/15 hole course at Son Parc (see page 66) is open to visitors. t 971 18 88 75 w www.clubsonparc.com

Go-karting Beside the hippodrome on the Maó to Sant Lluís road, or at Castillo Menorca, on the main road from Ferreries to Ciutadella. Both are open all day.

Snooker There are two full-size snooker tables at **Scandals** restaurant in Es Castell. t 971 36 53 13 11.00–23.00

Tennis There are tennis-courts in the larger resorts and also in Maó.

Windsurfing – one of the exhilarating water sports on offer

Festivals & events

CONCERTS

Classical music lovers should look out for the international festivals held in Maó and Ciutadella in July and August – details of concerts can be found in local papers or on posters in the cities. There are also daily morning organ concerts from Monday to Saturday in the church of Santa Maria in Maó. The Teatro Principal (see page 15) in Maó has a variety of entertainment – see local press for details.

FESTIVALS

Every town in Menorca has its annual festival, in honour of its patron saint, with street parties, fireworks and displays of horse riding in the main square. Some of the largest festivals take place in Es Castell (24–26 July), Ferreries (23–25 August) and Maó (7–9 September), but the biggest and most colourful of all is the festival of Sant Joan (St John),

CALENDAR OF MAIN FESTIVALS	
Ciutadella	23 and 24 June
Es Castell	24–26 July
Fornells	4th weekend in July
Es Migjorn	Last weekend July/first in August
Alaior	First 2 weeks in August
San Clemente	3rd weekend in August
Ferrerias	23 and 24 Aug
Sant Lluís	End August
Maó	7–9 Sept
Cala en Porter	3rd weekend in September

◀ Flamenco dancers put on a thrilling display

held in Ciutadella on 23–25 June. It begins with a horseback procession and ends with a massive firework display in Plaça d'es Born, and in between are two days of riotous festivities, all fuelled by large amounts of *pomada* – gin with lemon.

HORSES

The Menorcan passion for horses can also be seen at the trotting races which take place each weekend at the racetracks outside Maó and Ciutadella. The jockey sits in a small cart behind the horse and his job is to make it go as fast as possible without breaking into a gallop. There is a fun family atmosphere and most people have a small bet on the horses. The races begin at around 18.00 in Maó on Saturdays and, in Ciutadella, at 18.00 on Sundays.

JAZZ

One of the places to hear live jazz is at Casino de San Clemente, on the main street of San Clemente, from 21.30 on Tuesdays (see page 34). Jazzbah, in Ciutadella also has live music (see page 92).

MUSIC & FOLK DANCING

A lively display of local music and dancing is usually on offer at weekends in main towns and resorts. See local press for details.

Club Escola Menorquina, on the road from Ferreries to Cala Galdana, gives twice-weekly demonstrations of typically Menorcan dressage skills at their riding stables (see page 83). During the interval, there are donkey rides for the children.

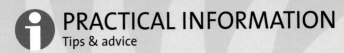

Preparing to go

GETTING THERE

The cheapest way to get to Menorca is to book a package holiday with one of the leading tour operators specialising in Spanish island holidays. If your travelling times are flexible, and if you can avoid the school holidays, you can also find some very cheap last-minute deals using the websites for the leading holiday companies.

BY AIR

The majority of visitors use charter companies to get to Menorca, which operate from nearly all of the UK's regional airports. Menorca's modern airport is also served by scheduled international flights from the UK and by internal flights from Spanish airports at Madrid, Valencia and Barcelona. The airport can be reached on ☎ 971 15 70 00

SPANISH TOURIST OFFICE

Further information about Menorca can be obtained from the **Spanish Tourist Office**, PO Box 4009, London W1A 6NB ☎ 020 7486 8077
🖷 020 7486 8034 ❷ tourspain@latestinfo.co.uk ⓦ www.spain.info
🕘 Open 09.15–16.15, Mon–Fri

BEFORE YOU LEAVE

Holidays should be about fun and relaxation, so avoid last minute panics and stress by making your preparations well in advance.

It is not necessary to have inoculations to travel in Europe, but you should make sure you and your family are up to date with the basics, such as tetanus. It is a good idea to pack a small first-aid kit to carry with you containing plasters, antiseptic cream, travel sickness pills, insect repellent and/or bite-relief cream, antihistamine tablets, upset stomach remedies and painkillers. Sun lotion can be more expensive in many holiday destinations than in the UK so it is worth taking a good selection especially of the higher factor lotions if you have children with you. If you are taking prescription medicines, ensure that you take enough for the duration of your visit – you may find it difficult to obtain the same medicines in Menorca. It is also worth having a dental check-up before you go.

DOCUMENTS

The most important documents you will need are your tickets and your passport. Check well in advance that your passport is up to date and has at least three months left to run (six months is even better). All children, including newborn babies, need their own passport now. It generally takes at least three weeks to process a passport renewal. This can be longer in the run-up to the summer months.

Contact the **Passport Agency** for the latest information on how to renew your passport and what the processing times are likely to be. ☎ 0870 521 0410 Ⓦ www.ukpa.gov.uk.

You should check the details of your travel tickets well before your departure, ensuring that the timings and dates are correct.

If you are thinking of hiring a car while you are away, you will need to have your UK driving licence with you. If you want more than one driver for the car, the other drivers must have their licences too.

MONEY

You will need some currency before you go, especially if your flight gets you to your destination at the weekend or late in the day after the banks have closed. Travellers' cheques are the safest way to carry money because the money will be refunded if the cheques are lost or stolen. To buy travellers' cheques or exchange money at a bank you may need to give up to a week's notice, depending on the quantity of foreign currency you require. You can exchange money at the airport before you depart. You should also make sure that your credit, charge and debit cards are up to date – you do not want them to expire mid-holiday – and that your credit limit is sufficient to allow you to make those holiday purchases. Once you arrive, you will find cash dispensers in all the resorts. Do not forget, too, to check your PIN numbers in case you have not used them for a while – you may want to draw money while you are away. Ring your bank or card company and they will help you out.

INSURANCE

Check that your policy covers you adequately for loss of possessions and valuables, for activities you might want to try – such as scuba-diving, horse riding, or water sports – and for emergency medical and dental treatment, including flights home if required.

It is essential to take an E111 form (available from post offices) with you, to ensure that if you have any medical treatment while away you can reclaim the costs on your return. After January 2006, a new EHIC card replaces the E111 form to allow UK visitors access to reduced-cost and sometimes free state-provided medical treatment in the EEA. For further information, ring EHIC enquiries line. ☎ 0845 605 0707 or visit the Department of Health website: ⓦ www.dh.gov.uk

CLIMATE

Average monthly temperatures on Menorca:

Month	Temp ºC	Humidity %	Rainfall mm	Daily hours of sunshine
Jan	8–14	77	64	3.5
Feb	8–14	76	49	4.5
Mar	8–16	76	50	6
April	10–18	77	47	7
May	13–21	71	30	8.5
June	17–25	67	19	10
July	20–28	65	7	11
Aug	21–29	68	30	10
Sept	18–26	73	70	7
Oct	15–22	75	105	6
Nov	11–18	77	92	4
Dec	8–15	77	85	3

Source: Centro Meteorologico Zonal, Palma de Mallorca

July and August can be very hot and it can be difficult to sleep at night. Many hotels have air-conditioning, but it's worth checking before booking. Loose clothes made from natural fibres are the best to wear.

PETS

Remember to make arrangements for the care of your pets while you are away – book them into a reputable cat or dog hotel, or make arrangements with a trustworthy neighbour to ensure that they are properly fed, watered and exercised while you are on holiday.

SECURITY

Take sensible precautions to prevent your house being burgled while you are away:

- Cancel milk, newspapers and other regular deliveries so that post and milk does not pile up on the doorstep, indicating that you are away.
- Let the postman know where to leave parcels and bulky mail that will not go through your letterbox (ideally with a next-door neighbour).
- If possible, arrange for a friend or neighbour to visit regularly, closing and opening your curtains, and switching the lights on and off, giving the impression that there is someone living in the house.
- Consider buying electrical timing devices that will switch lights and radios on and off.
- Let Neighbourhood Watch representatives know that you will be away so that they can keep an eye on your home.
- If you have a burglar alarm, make sure that it is serviced and working properly and is switched on when you leave (you may find that your insurance policy requires this). Ensure that a neighbour is able to gain access to the alarm to turn it off if it is set off accidentally.
- If you are leaving cars unattended, put them in a garage, if possible, and leave a key with a neighbour in case the alarm goes off.

TELEPHONING MENORCA
To call Menorca from the UK, dial 00 34 followed by the nine-digit number.

AIRPORT PARKING & ACCOMMODATION

If you intend to leave your car in an airport car park while you are away, or stay the night at an airport hotel before or after your flight, you should book well ahead to take advantage of discounts or cheap off-airport parking. Airport accommodation gets booked up several weeks in advance, especially during the height of the holiday season. Check whether the hotel offers free parking for the duration of the holiday – often the savings made on parking costs can significantly reduce the accommodation price.

BAGGAGE ALLOWANCE

Baggage allowances vary according to the airline, destination and the class of travel, but 20 kg (44 lb) per person is the norm for luggage that is carried in the hold (it usually tells you what the weight limit is on your ticket). You are also allowed one item of cabin baggage weighing no more than 5 kg (11 lb) and measuring 46 by 30 by 23 cm (18 by 12 by 9 inches). In addition, you can usually carry your duty-free purchases, umbrella, handbag, coat, camera, etc, as hand baggage. Large items – surfboards, golf-clubs, collapsible wheelchairs and pushchairs – are usually charged as extras and it is a good idea to let the airline know in advance that you want to bring these.

CHECK-IN, PASSPORT CONTROL AND CUSTOMS

First-time travellers can often find airport security intimidating, but it is all very easy really.

Check-in desks usually open two or three hours before the flight is due to depart. Arrive early for the best choice of seats and look for your flight number on the TV monitors in the check-in area to find the relevant check-in desk. At the desk, your tickets will be checked and your luggage weighed and taken on board.

Take your boarding card and go to the departure gate. Here your hand luggage will be X-rayed and your passport checked. In the departure area, you can shop and relax but keep an eye on the monitors that tell you when to board – usually about 30 minutes before take-off.

Go to the departure gate shown on the monitor and follow the instructions given to you by the airline staff to board your flight.

During your stay

AIRPORTS
Depending on your flight time and day of travel the airport on Menorca can be very busy. It only needs two or three flights to be delayed before the departure lounge becomes overcrowded. Make sure you have water to drink and something to eat, especially if you are travelling with children. There are places to buy food and drink at the airport but the queues can be long. There are a number of airport shops selling products from alcohol, cigarettes and perfume to locally-produced goods such as shoes, cheese and jewellery.

BEACHES
In summer, the most popular beaches usually have life guards on duty and/or a flag safety system. Make sure you know and understand what the various flags mean and never swim after drinking alcohol or when a red flag is flying. Other beaches may be safe for swimming but there are unlikely to be lifeguards or life-saving amenities available. Bear in mind that the strong winds that develop in the hotter months can quickly change a safe beach into a not-so-safe one, and some can have strong currents the further out that you go. If in doubt, ask your local representative or at your hotel.

> **BEACH SAFETY**
> A flag system is used to warn bathers when sea conditions are unsafe for swimming.
> - Red (or black): dangerous – no swimming
> - Yellow: good swimmers only – apply caution
> - Green (or white): safe bathing conditions for all

CHILDREN'S ACTIVITIES

Most hotels have a club for children and it's a good idea to try and take advantage of these. They are well organised and offer a wide range of activities. The day usually finishes with a mini-disco. If you are not in a hotel there is usually a centre nearby where it is safe for children to play and these centres often offer organised games. There are, of course, the many wonderful beaches around the island. Some are safer than others for children: always check locally before allowing children into the water and supervise them at all times.

CONSULATE

The Honorary British Vice-Consul is based at Sa Casa Nova, Cami de Biniatap 30, Horizonte ☎ 971 363373 ❶ 971 35 46 90

CURRENCY

The currency in Menorca is the euro (€). The note denominations are 500, 200, 100, 50, 20. 10 and 5 euro . The euro is divided into cents, with 1, 2, 5, 10, 20 and 50 cent coins.

> The higher exchange rate is only a good deal if the commission charged is not excessive.

CUSTOMS & FESTIVALS

During the summer months each town celebrates its own festivals. These are very noisy occasions with parades of giants, various musical events from folk dancing to pop groups and spectacular firework displays. The most traditional is the *jaleo* where rearing horses move through the crowd. It is considered good luck to touch the horse when it is rearing; only the brave try this. Menorca is the only place in Spain where you can see the *jaleo*, the most famous being the festival in Ciutadella in which up to 150 horses take part. One *jaleo* takes place at night with another the following midday (see page 107 for calendar of main festivals).

DRESS CODES

Menorcans are basically Catholic, and will be offended by beachwear worn in the towns. It is respectful to them to cover up when leaving the beach and by not wearing skimpy shorts and tops, or no shirt when going into town. The beach dress code is absolutely fine, however, for the holiday resorts.

ELECTRICITY

Menorca has the same voltage as the UK, but with two-pin plugs, so you will need to bring an adaptor. These are readily available in the UK at electrical shops or major chemists. If you are considering buying electrical appliances to take home, always check that they will work in the UK before you buy them.

FACILITIES FOR THE DISABLED

On the whole Menorca is a disabled-friendly island with easy access to most facilities. Most pavements are also adapted for wheelchairs. Some beaches have good access but possibly not toilet facilities nearby. There are taxis for disabled use but you must request these.

GETTING AROUND

Buses From the bus station in Maó buses run six times daily along the main road from Maó to Ciutadella. There are also bus services from Maó to Es Castell, Sant Lluís, Binibeca, Es Canutells, Cala'n Porter, Son Bou, Cala Galdana, Arenal d'en Castell, Son Parc and Fornells, and from Ciutadella to Cala Galdana, Cala'n Bosch, Sa Caleta and Cala'n Forcat.

Taxis These are available in all of the main resorts. The taxis are not metered, so you should check the fare in advance. Drivers keep a list of fares for the most common routes and you can ask to see this. A tip is always welcome!

Hiring a car There are car hire offices in all the main resorts – the biggest local company is Betacar. To hire a car you need your driving licence and you should keep this on you at all times, along with the hire documents and a copy of your passport. There are several petrol stations around Maó and Ciutadella and along the main road between the two, but few on the rest of the island so it is worth keeping the tank topped up. 🕐 Most petrol stations are open 07.00–21.00 and a few are open 24 hours. Most of the others have self-service machines outside these hours where you can pay for your petrol in advance using Spanish banknotes. All hire cars take the unleaded petrol known as Eurosuper, or *sin plomo*.

RULES OF THE ROAD

The speed limits are 55mph (90km/h) on the main highway, 30mph (50km/h) in towns and 20mph (30km/h) on country roads, unless indicated otherwise. These are strictly enforced, as are the drink-driving laws (it is illegal to drink alcohol and drive). Children must sit in the back and young children need a special seat – tell the hire firm if you need one (some firms charge extra for this). Seat belts must be worn at all times.

Useful words for drivers
- *aparcamiento* parking
- *estacionamiento prohibido* no parking
- *ceda al paso* give way to the right and left
- *circunvalación* ring road

HEALTH MATTERS

Health hazards People who are not used to the sun burn easily – and children are especially vulnerable. It is a good idea to cover up with a strong sunblock, wear a hat and keep out of the midday sun. In a hot climate you also need to drink a lot more fluids.

Water The tap water is safe to drink but can be very salty. Mineral water is widely available and cheap.

Chemists Easily recognized by the big green cross above the door with the word 'Farmacia', chemists are very good on the island, supplying everything you might need including antibiotics, which you can buy over the counter. The staff are helpful and knowledgeable – if you want something not in stock, they will normally try to get it for you. There are also chemists open 24 hours by rota (posted on all chemist doors).

Medical treatment If you have medical insurance or are willing to pay, you can contact the private **Salus Health Clinic**. The lines are open 24 hours a day and the staff speak English. The freephone number is 🛈 900 60 50 50. Dental treatment is not usually covered by insurance, but in an emergency contact Salus health clinic on the same number.

EMERGENCY TELEPHONE NUMBERS
The general emergency telephone number is **112**
You can call an ambulance on **061** and the police on **091**

THE LANGUAGE

Since 1983 the official language of Menorca has been Catalan, but Spanish is also widely spoken and many people speak English and German, especially in the resorts. The change from Spanish to Catalan in recent years has been very gradual, and street signs are in either Spanish or Catalan. The people of Menorca speak Menorquín (the dialect of Catalan spoken on Menorca) rather than Spanish, and they are proud of the difference between the two languages. The capital, Maó, is known as Mahón in Spanish; Ciutadella is known as Ciudadela.

ENGLISH	SPANISH (pronunciation)
General vocabulary	
yes	*sí* (see)
no	*no* (no)
please	*por favor* (por faBOR)
thank you (very much)	*(muchas) gracias* ((MOOchas) GRAseeyas)
you're welcome	*de nada* (deNAda)
hello	*hola* (Ola)
goodbye	*adiós* (adeeYOS)
good morning/day	*buenos días* (BWEnos DEEyas)

ENGLISH	SPANISH (pronunciation)

General vocabulary (continued)

good afternoon/evening	*buenas tardes* (BWEnas TARdes)
good evening (after dark)	*buenas noches* (BWEnas NOches)
excuse me (to get attention or to get past)	*¡disculpe!* (desKOOLpay)
excuse me (to apologize or to ask pardon)	*¡perdón!* (perDON)
sorry	*lo siento* (lo seeYENtoe)
Help!	*¡socorro!* (SOHcohroe)
	¡ayuda! (aiYUda)
today	*hoy* (oy)
tomorrow	*mañana* (manYAna)
yesterday	*ayer* (ayYER)

Useful words and phrases

open	*abierto* (abeeYERtoe)
closed	*cerrado* (serRAdoe)
push	*empujar* (empooHA)
pull	*tirar* (teeRAR)
How much is it?	*¿Cuánto es?* (KWANtoe es)
expensive	*caro/a* (KARo/a)
bank	*el banco* (el BANko)
bureau de change	*la oficina de cambio* (la ofeeSEEna de KAMbeeyo)
post office	*correos* (koRAYos)
duty (all-night) chemist	*la farmacia de guardia* (la farMAHseeya de garDEEya)
bank card	*la tarjeta de banco* (la tarHEHta deBANko)
credit card	*la tarjeta de crédito* (la tarHEHta de CREdeetoe)
traveller's cheques	*los cheques de viaje* (los CHEkes de beeAhay)

ENGLISH	SPANISH (pronunciation)
Useful words and phrases (continued)	
table	*la mesa* (la MEHsa)
menu	*el menú/la carta* (el menOO/la KARta)
waiter	*el/la camarero/a* (el/la kahmahRERo/a)
water	*agua* (Agwa)
fizzy/still water	*agua con/sin gas* (Agwa con/sin gas)
I don't understand	*No entiendo* (No enteeYENdoe)
The bill, please	*La cuenta, por favor* (la KWENta, porfaBOR)
Do you speak English?	*¿Habla usted inglés?* (Ablah OOsted eenGLES)
My name is...	*Me llamo ...* (meh YAmoh ...)
Where are the toilets?	*¿Dónde están los servicios?* (DONdeh esTAN los serVEEseeos)
Can you help me?	*¿Puede ayudarme?* (PWEday ayooDARmeh)
Where are the toilets?	*¿Dónde están los servicios?* (DONdeh esTAN los serVEEseeos)
Can you call me a taxi?	*¿Puede llamar a un taxi?* (PWEday yaMAR ah oon TAKsee)

MEDIA

A good selection of English newspapers can be bought in the resorts, the more popular ones being printed in Spain. Many popular English magazines can also be easily found. The larger supermarkets have an excellent selection of newspapers and magazines for all ages. Most hotels have satellite television so you can watch your favourite programmes in English. Most British-owned bars and restaurants have satellite television and usually organise a special night if there is an important event on TV.

OPENING HOURS

Banks ● Mon–Fri 08.30–14.15

Shops 🕐 Mon–Fri 09.30–13.30 and 17.30–20.30, Sat 09.30–13.30
These are times for shops in towns. Local shops in resorts may open all day – consult individual shops for opening times

Supermarkets 🕐 Mon–Sat 09.00–21.00, Sun 09.00–14.00 (however, not all supermarkets are open on Sunday)

Churches All towns have at least one **Roman Catholic** church. The times of services and Mass are usually posted on the door. The **Anglican Church**, Santa Margarita, is in Calle Stuart, Es Castell. Services are: Sunday 09.00 and 11.00, Wednesday 11.00, and Friday (healing service) 11.00. For services in Ciutadella contact the chaplain (🕐 971 35 23 78). The **Evangelical Church** in Es Castell has a service Sunday 11.30; in Maó Sunday 10.00 and 18.00.

PERSONAL COMFORT AND SECURITY

Making a complaint Many restaurants and hotels have a book for official complaints. Nevertheless it is usually better to speak to the manager to try to sort the problem out first hand.

Laundry and dry cleaning If you are not in an hotel, or do not want to use the hotel's laundry service, there are dry cleaners (*tintoreria*) in most main towns.

Public toilets There are no public toilets in towns except in bars. It is normal to use these without purchasing anything though it is considered polite if you do.

Lost property Your insurance company will require you to go to the local police to report anything valuable which has been lost or stolen. The police are very helpful. Keep the original version and photocopies of any official forms or documents the police require you to fill out and sign.

POST OFFICES

Many shops selling postcards will have stamps too. Opening hours in the main towns are:

Maó 🕐 Mon–Fri 09.00-21.00 and Sat 09.00-14.00
Ciutadella 🕐 Mon–Fri 09.00-19.00 and Sat 09.00-14.00

Post offices in other towns have their own opening hours. Consult each office for times. Stamps can usually be bought where postcards are sold.

TELEPHONES
Phone kiosks are everywhere, with instructions in several languages. Phonecards are available in post offices and shops for €6 or €12. You can also use your credit card in most public phones. Some bars and kiosks have metered phones where you can make your call first and pay for it afterwards. Cheap rate is from 22.00 to 08.00 and on Sundays and official fiestas. Local calls are very cheap. Remember to dial the local code for the Balearic Islands (971) before each number (as listed in this book).

TIME DIFFERENCE
Menorca is one hour ahead of British time.

TIPPING
A service charge of 10 per cent is normally added to restaurant bills, but a tip of an additional 5 to 10 per cent can be left at your discretion. If you are just having a drink in a bar, leave some loose change. Up to 10 per cent is acceptable as a tip for taxi drivers and a tour guide should be given €1.

WEIGHTS & MEASUREMENTS
The metric system is used, as in the UK:

Imperial to metric	Metric to imperial
1 inch = 2.54 centimetres	1 centimetre = 0.4 inches
1 foot = 30 centimetres	1 metre = 3 feet, 3 inches
1 mile = 1.6 kilometres	1 kilometre = 0.6 miles
1 ounce = 28 grams	1 gram = 0.04 ounces
1 pound = 454 grams	1 kilogram = 2.2 pounds
1 pint = 0.6 litres	1 litre = 1.8 pints
1 gallon = 4.6 litres	

CLOTHING SIZES
Women's clothing

British	10	12	14	16	18	20
European	40	42	44	46	48	50

Men's clothing

British	36	38	40	42	44	46
European	46	48	50	52	54	56

Shirts

British	14	14½	15	15½	16	16½
European	36	37	38	39	41	42

Shoes

British	3	3½	4	5	6	7	7½	8	9	10
European	35	36	37	38	39	40	41	42	43	44

TELEPHONING ABROAD
The dialling code for international access is 00.
Wait until a second dialling tone is heard, then dial the country code (UK = 44), followed by the area code (without the initial zero) and the subscriber number.

INDEX

ACKNOWLEDGEMENTS

We would like to thank all the photographers, picture libraries and organizations for the loan of the photographs reproduced in this book, to whom copyright in the photograph belongs:
Teresa Fisher (pages 8, 69, 10, 17, 20–1, 28, 72, 75, 85);
Foto Dolfo (page 23);
Jupiter Images Corporation (pages 108, 125);
Pictures Colour Library Ltd (pages 53, 93, 94);
Thomas Cook Tour Operations Ltd (pages 1, 5, 13, 15, 31, 33, 43, 40–1, 47, 55, 61, 63, 67, 76, 89, 90, 101, 102, 105, 106,).

We would also like to thank the following for their contribution to this series:
John Woodcock (map and symbols artwork);
Becky Alexander, Patricia Baker, Sophie Bevan, Judith Chamberlain-Webber, Stephanie Evans, Nicky Gyopari, Krystyna Mayer, Robin Pridy (editorial support);
Christine Engert, Suzie Johanson, Richard Lloyd, Richard Peters, Alistair Plumb, Jane Prior, Barbara Theisen, Ginny Zeal, Barbara Zuñiga (design support).

Send your thoughts to
books@thomascook.com

- Found a beach bar, peaceful stretch of sand or must-see sight that we don't feature?
- Like to tip us off about any information that needs a little updating?
- Want to tell us what you love about this handy, little guidebook and more importantly how we can make it even handier?

Then here's your chance to tell all! Send us ideas, discoveries and recommendations today and then look out for your valuable input in the next edition of this title. And, as an extra 'thank you' from Thomas Cook Publishing, you'll be automatically entered into our exciting monthly prize draw.

Send an email to the above address or write to:
HotSpots Project Editor, Thomas Cook Publishing, PO Box 227, Unit 15/16, Coningsby Road, Peterborough PE3 8SB, UK.